Journey in the Mind's Eye of a Poet: A Search for Faith

BOOK TWO (2006 TO 2008)

Portals and Passages

Burdens of Secrets Kept

Tony Prewit

Journey in the Mind's Eye of a Poet: A Search for Faith
Book Two (2006 to 2008): Portals and Passages

copyright Tony Prewit, 2012

Published by Ridgeline Press
Silver City, New Mexico, U.S.A.
ISBN 978-0-9854487-1-4

Editing, book design, cover design, and production services by
Heidi Connolly, Harvard Girl Word Services
Cover artwork by Tony Prewit

Acknowledgments

I would like to thank my wife, Patricia Prewit, for the years of assistance in sorting, editing, and proofreading all my work. I thank her most of all for her being her and allowing me to continue to be the person she married. I would also like to thank Sarah Johnson, a professional proofreader, who offered intelligent suggestions in shaping these books and gave me a valuable critique of its quality and content. Finally, I would like to thank the friends who read the complete series, contributed valuable suggestions, and urged me to arrange it into the form it has become: Gretchen Van Auken, Charlie Mckee, and Gail Rein. I thank Raymond Hornbaker for the years of commitment to our late-night discussions. I would also like to mention the editor who helped with the final sculpture of these books, Heidi Connolly, whose vision, talent, and professional guidance have been invaluable.

Burdens of Secrets Kept

1.

Secrets kept can be peace or burden
Who is to know but the bearer?
Kept secrets too long inside
ached at my soul wanting out
as I lived a religion I did not believe
keeping secrets for the sake
of keeping the friends who believed
what I had silently rejected

Secrets outed have since caused some
to disdain my presence
though no harm had I done
except not to believe in God as they.

2.

And what of the secret dreams and voices
I have heard since my youth
those which have conversed with me
for as long as I can remember?
My rejected religion considered them
a subject not to be discussed
lest I would hear of my error

Still I journeyed with these voices and dreams
learning their ways and their origins
and the secrets became like jewels to me
though I was shunned by the followers
of the religion that failed me

I am known by them as one who possesses voices
and as a liar to God forsaking faith

Yet a calm rest has come upon me
since my secrets have been set free

Unburdened I journey my own way
to speak what I believe
and to live with the voices I hear
as they pass through my soul
and on to their destination.

> *— the value of the burdens of secrets kept*
> *what others called error became the lessons learned.*

Table of Contents

Prologue

These six books are written in a poetry/prose form, a process that spans thirty-five years and encompasses the gradual evolution into my inner search for a personal faith and belief in God. It is a poet's journal and also like a novel in poetry form, one in which I am the narrator as well as a main character. The poems document my gradual disengagement with traditional, conservative, evangelical Christianity as I built a belief and faith of my own. Although I certainly did not have this defined purpose when I started this journal, it matured this way over time to become collection of six books that record a journey in search of a faith I could call my own.

As I walk away from the Christianity in which I once believed without doubting the existence of a God, I continue to discover a place within where I am learning how to build my own faith. This writing is for those who are at a dead end or a crossroad in their belief, or in a dysfunctional relationship (so to speak) with their spiritual beliefs. One of my messages, therefore, is that our spiritual beliefs do not have to be unchangeable.

Consequently, these poems are not so much a criticism of Christianity as they are a process of learning to ask the right questions. Over time I have learned to be wary of those who do not want to hear my questions and who are defensive toward honest doubt and inquiry. Because I was trapped in a doctrine that did not allow me to express my belief in my own way, and because I wanted to keep my Christian friends, I kept silent for many years.

The poems in this work capture my observations and reflections about how I see life through the veil of my own struggle, and will hopefully allow others to consider the shortcomings of their own beliefs, or of any belief that does not allow for true dialog. Because none of us really knows the truth for sure when it comes to belief, it would appear that there are shortcomings in all spiritual belief systems, regardless of form. For that reason, we are left to ourselves to construct a satisfactory — and satisfying — faith.

The stunning effect of this pursuit is my finding that God gets larger from the inside out. This is where my journey has found its pleasure and its peace, even while admitting the sorrow and fear of the search.

I have wrestled with my soul along this path and it wrestled back, for what I was struggling with was my spiritual identity. In wrestling, I learned the value of putting forth the right questions rather than assuming I had the right answers.

In fact, questions have become answers in their own right for me, for a light turned on in the asking that helped illuminate my way. I further learned that without questions we have no way to really appreciate where we are going and why. As such, I am thankful that I realized the importance of questions within the arena of spiritual beliefs.

The six books in this series are (in order): *Journal of Time*, *Portals and Passages*, *The Book of the Lost and Found* or *Chasing Rainbows*, *Moods of War*, *The Source*, and *Another Day*.

Book One is the beginning of my realizations and observations of life, which I describe as "me looking inside me from the perspective of the outside me," and then, "me looking outside me from the perspective of the inside me." It is the discovery of my need for a faith in God of my own. Book Two is a confession of my dreams and the effect dreams can have upon one's life. Book Two also reveals my earliest thoughts concerning my spiritual beliefs, kept very secret until then, and how these secrets became a burden to my search for faith. In Books Three and Four I begin to focus my writing toward a more intense spiritual inquiry based on my discontentment with religious answers. These two works became like a great mountain I needed to climb, blocking the path of what I considered my "true" journey. One might also describe them as an inner wrestling match where the rule was to fight to the finish. In total these books are the recording of how I lost my past faith and discovered what I call "conflicts of faith." Hence, Book Five is the result of feeling as if I had reached the top of the mountain, had a good view of a long way down the road, and could tell that although the journey was long from over, I was sensing a peace that came from finding my own faith. Book Six is about learning to live with the faith I had created.

Phrases and Words

The phrase "Treat others as we want them to treat us" is the most frequently used phrase in these books, and it has become more important to me as the years have passed. It has become a part of the foundation of my own faith because no matter how I might try, it stuck with me, withstanding all inquiry, doubt, and question.

To treat others as we want them to treat us simply means to me that we value others as equal to ourselves and value their needs as important as our own. And that if we do not wish to be cheated, lied to, deceived, oppressed, or manipulated, then we should be willing not to cheat, lie, deceive, oppress, or manipulate others.

I use other Judeo-Christian terms such as "heaven" and "hell" and the duality of "good" and "evil." These terms and their meanings come from my own culture and western traditional Christian teaching. I do not necessarily consider these terms to be universally accepted as truth; they serve only as my own points of reference into my inner spiritual search.

My use of the word "God" in the masculine form is habit and based somewhat on the limitations of the English language. In my mind, God is of no gender, no religion, no race, no culture.

In some parts you may find the writing in these books somewhat redundant. The repetitiveness serves as an accurate picture of my perspective, however, for I believe we are all in the process of being formed and we repeat our thoughts and feelings until they either become a part of us or fade.

My style of writing is varied. It weaves poetry, commentary, and prose. I do not attempt to stay inside the lines of strict grammatical compliance. I give myself poetic license. I am much more concerned with content and the work's original form than with adherence to rules. You'll see I have also invented a few words along the way.

Initially, my poetry/journal was not produced as a neat stack of notebooks; instead, scattered notebooks, legal pads, single sheets, and scratch paper filled with writings piled up until the notebooks piled up on top of each other. They were in no real order. No, I did not have a neat stack at all. In fact, after thirty-five years' worth of notebooks had turned into a kind of organizational nightmare, I felt it was almost futile to even attempt to sort through it all. Common sense prevailed, however, and this six-book format is the result of sorting and compiling a presentable record of my writings.

Introduction (Three Poems)

1. Journey in the Mind's Eye of a Poet

The journey in the mind's eye of a poet
is the journey to the rooms of the soul
where the spirit dwells and where
the voices of the spirits are heard

It is there I discover
the voice of my own spirit
and voices not my own
as if all living things have a spirit
and a voice to share

Were we made to hear the voices of all these living things?
Were we made to speak to all the living things through
our voice?

> *I dwell in the rooms of your soul*
> *and for all who can hear:*
> *beware of other voices knocking*
> *at the doors of your soul*
>
> *There are thousands of windows*
> *portals and passages*
> *and thousands of rooms and doors*

There are many who hear and obey the voices
that travel through the portals and passages
of the seen and unseen world of the soul
Some voices are evil some are good
One voice is our own

I listen for my own voice
and I listen for another

He says to me, "listen and discern of My voice
Beware of which voice you are willing to follow,
for there are many."

This voice of which I speak is not heard as other voices
I believe it has no words to speak
It is we who must sense its presence and learn the way

I fear we confuse all these other voices with this One.

2. Destined to It

An unusual quietness came upon me suddenly
The noise of the day seemed to fade
I began to listen without knowing exactly why
more of a reaction than a response
The words I place on my lips now are the same words
I heard

I come not to make governments, nor money for men
I come to prepare them for eternity
Tell them

The earth was given to you to do with as you will
You have caused the fights and so you must cause the peace

I am not of you; I am only passing through

Without another sound the quietness faded
The noise of the day resumed
To live with unusual sensations such as these

Is like a test of my most inner parts
Who would believe me or take it seriously?

3. Entry One

i usually wake early
around 4:00 to 4:30 a.m.
i don't think it means anything
spiritual or wise
it is just when i naturally awaken
it is my own rhythm
and i accept it

many mornings i lie in bed
for a few minutes
and listen to my wife's
steady rhythmic breathing as she sleeps
she wakes later than i do
it is her rhythm and
we allow each other our own

i thought it was a good idea to mention
my early rising and my wife
so you would know
that i do rise early and
that it does our marriage good
when we allow each other
such personal things.

Part One:
I Am Not One of You

What Is This I Speak

Abraham announced
I am a stranger in a strange land

Jesus proclaimed
I only do what I see the Father doing
Where I go you cannot go

And a voice in me makes known my own revelation
I am not one of you
I am only passing through.

Unwelcome Spirits

the silence of the morning
awakens all the visitors in my soul
it's time for you to get up and get out
i will not share my house with you

the first breeze at dawn
is the alarm before the light goes on
today is house-cleaning day
    no doubt some will seek the dark corners

as the sun looks over the hills
the unwelcome are seeking cover
the broom is busy sweeping
    and the trash is being tossed out

thus the day begins as every day
with the rustling of my spirit
to clean its house and sweep its soul clean
    unwelcome spirits know when they are not welcome

    unwelcome spirit fear mine own
    – for i have given my soul to my God
    and my God is jealous over His house.

I Am Not One of You Revelation (The Coming-out Party)

I stand in the midst of a gathering of friends, feeling somewhat alone and out of place. From inside me, I see my past and present as if I am standing before God, asking myself, what the reason is for my loneliness.

In a dark corner of my mind a knowing comes to the surface, as if some distant truth far inside my memory is coming as a revelation, whispering to me, and interrupting my thoughts without regard to this gathering of friends.

The memories I have of these friends are being pushed against by this new revelation. I hear the voices of my friends come and then fade, loud and then soft. Their images disappear as the new revelation invades my thoughts.

A confession deep inside me wants to say to this gathering, "Though we have shared many times together, there will be always a distance between us. We are as close as we can get, and it seems the gap between us will not be closed."

The memories of you can be described as if I am traveling down a road and seeking direction for my journey. You have always been there, but now I know you cannot journey with me any farther or, if you do, you will not journey far.

I see a sign at a distance and cannot yet read it, and a despair overcomes me. The familiar voices of friends are like a voice calling me home for dinner. Their calling is now faint and too far away to guide me home. I stray farther from the voices of the familiar, being drawn by a new voice, a new revelation of truth, luring me, whispering to me the secrets that have been there all along.

I am looking through a tunnel and time seems to stop
The revelation in me demands to be known
In the silence I can hear it screaming, "Time to come out"
Like the coming of age like the coming-out party
A voice that has always been is ready now
For the first time it makes itself known

So as I stand in this crowded room silently
I am being confirmed as to who I am and who I am not
No one knows what has just happened And beyond it
there seems no rule

My silent voice quietly sends its message out
to everyone around me, whoever can hear, it says,

"I am not one of you, I am only passing through"

This happened inside me one night
If you have experienced it something like it
you will know it is quite the victory.

Watching Me

as a child i looked out a window
and saw me looking at me
saw myself playing

the memory of it is clear
from where did this memory come
seeing myself
knowing i was observing myself
knowing that it is an odd thing
to watch yourself from a window
playing outside

perhaps it is just an unexplainable memory
though a curious one
a memory from a place deep inside me
wanting recognition

as i watched me as i played outside
i thought i was different from the others around me

a feeling passed over me
a feeling without words
a feeling that resembled this

   "i am not one of you; i am only passing through."

Another Memory of Watching Me

i am sitting in the reverend's office of the methodist church
being coached for my baptism
i am eleven years old
it was my idea

i tell my parents i want to be baptized
they are somewhat puzzled
as if the pamphlet on child-rearing
should have mentioned this
but they agree

so i sit with the methodist reverend
a large man with large hands
the smell of the room is of old books
adobe walls and wood floors

it was as if i had been told beforehand
and was supposed to remember it
when the time was right
so i was baptized at eleven
and walked through the motions

as all the grownups stood in line
to congratulate me for the fine baptism
a feeling passed over me without words
if there had been words they would have been
"i am not one of you; i am only passing through"

though i was very young
the whole of this memory
was like me watching me
going through a motion
i was supposed to go through

i did not feel i fit in then
and i do not feel i fit in now
        why?
i suspect there are volumes of books on this subject

i have experienced these impressions
        again and again and again

i imagine that many people have had unusual
        impressions such as these

i am just part of that crowd
        taking time now to have my say in this matter

my memory reminds me that these impressions
        started way back – before my birth.

I Am Not One of You

i saw a man standing before a gathering
and he was speaking to them
>i am not one of you
>i am only passing through
>i will share what i have because where i go
>i will not have need of it

the crowd pushed and shoved
they would have none of it
better to silence this man than allow him to speak to us
of an unknown or new truth that we eschew

and another voice unheard by the crowd
save by those who had the spiritual ears to hear it
proclaimed this message

>see the storm on the horizon
>is it your soul that stirs the wind
>and causes you such chaos
>determined not to give in

the wise man passed through the crowd untouched
the crowd could not possess him for their own
nor could they tolerate to hear him and so they
would never know the beauty of his words

while he is near take note and remember what he said
>go and do likewise
>— treat others the way you want to be treated

as the voice began to fade a question came to me:
how is it a man can be a servant and also determine his
destiny?

see the storm on the horizon
is it your soul that stirs the wind
and causes you such chaos
determined not to give in

i wake suddenly as if i were wrong to dream such a thing
and wrong to be so lazy in the afternoon.

A Not-one-of-you Confession

I joined you at the pew
raised my hands with you
walked with you in aisles of the churches
enjoyed your company and your smiles
I have no animosity or attachment to you

Though I believe your friendships are genuine
I must leave you now and walk a different path
that calls me
The strangeness of this confession
is like believing in fairies — only as an adult

>   *I am not one of you*
>   *I am only passing through*

My heart aches,
the secrets I have kept from you rubbing my emotions raw
all the while trying to believe as you would have me believe
I have given you many hours of smiles
but now I have only an empty stare

My secrets are coming to haunt me
Will I dare to speak my heart?
Will I live my life as I see it
or will my secrets be stored in an old trunk
in some forgotten attic?
Though my heart aches I am also at peace
for a decision has been made

>   *I am not one of you*
>   *I am only passing through*

It is not farewell
It is my journey that calls
Though I will not walk with you in these church halls
I will always hold your friendship close to me
Hence my fear now whether I have what it takes
to be shunned by you and your beliefs

Is there room on the Rock for me?
A journey like this for me is as real as the sacrament
you swallow each Sunday
Who shall decide reality and truth for another?
Not you and not me

It is not farewell
Perhaps it is grace I seek from you

I ask this: *Is your grace strong enough to open your eyes to see
how great the Rock is — to allow room for the likes of you and me
and all other believers who disagree?*

My hope has only doubt that you will accept my call
to walk this journey that is in me
My message is that none of us have the complete truth and
doctrine of faith
and that there are none who can show it by
the example of his life
For the life we live is what we truly believe
and to me that is the proof of our belief

I think now you see that

> *I am not one of you*
> *I am only passing through.*

Note on Cows

as i passed a small herd of cattle
on a wilderness path
a bull with horns stared me down
i walked slowly
weaving through them

i thought to myself *i hope they know that*

    — i am not one of them, i am only passing through.

Note on One Lone Coyote and Me

there were five of us standing on the mountain ridge
watching a lone coyote with its tail between its legs
pass by a few feet away

there was something in the coyote's way that seemed to
say
     — i am not one of you, i am only passing through

we let the coyote pass of course
and can only hope he shows me the same courtesy
as we showed him this day

and that if i find myself in the midst of a pack of coyotes
i hope and pray they can read my thoughts
and will show me some courtesy and
let me continue.

     — i am not one of you, i am only passing through.

Alzheimer's Eyes

though all eyes are looking at you
nothing is getting through

in and out no telling when
the slow descent will end

all the tears of those
who love you will never cease

as if you never knew us
and we never knew you

what are we to do with all the memories
when the last years were so painful

though you are not with us you are not forgotten
though you are as a stranger you are also a parent
and a spouse

who is your family now
what memories do you have

one moment at a time is lost forever
tomorrow will be the same only less

till the last breath
the scenario will be repeated again and again

the prayer we have —
if you cannot be healed then pass on

looking through alzheimer's eyes
do you wonder to yourself *when did i die?*

as i look into your dazed eyes i can hear your spirit say
i am not one of you, i am only passing through.

Destined to Believe

i had a dream
i woke up after a long sleep
and there was no one to be seen
i stood in this small dark room
and then i was walking along a seashore
and then i was climbing a high peak

i could see from the top of the peak
that i was alone on an island
where the sun set and rose for many days
my thoughts of survival and life
of whether there is a God or not
and of who would help me

soon a ship came and rescued me
the captain proclaiming that God
had shown him i was on the island

over the course of the journey
the passengers began to expect me
to give praise to the captain for saving my life

i explained to them that i was already saved
and that no man had saved me
that it was the God that i came to believe in on the island
who saved me and not the captain

the captain spoke harshly of my reasoning
disappointed i could not give him the honor of the rescue
(in private i thanked the captain, but that was not enough
as he wanted me to thank him publicly)

the captain and the passengers
shunned me for the rest of the trip
the news spreading of how ungrateful i was
though i had thanked the captain and the crew aside
i could see it was not enough
for it was my loyalty the crew wanted
as the captain wanted recognition for all to see
that he was the instrument of God
who had delivered me home

i spoke to a crew member in secret
and explained to him that to me
men like the captain want men's praise
only as a show of their righteousness
which means their faith is driven by recognition
and the approval of others

i do not know if i know the God of the captain
but i do proclaim that the God i met on the island
required me not to offer such high praise to men

*i give testimony to beware of any man who will take praise that
belongs only to God and of those who deem themselves worthy to
sit at His side.*

Letter to Earth

1.

letter to earth from the human spirit

i am of God
sent here by God
and you also are of God
created by God
to receive me

i am in your land
by no decision of my own
that i am aware
sent here to stay
till further notice

forgive me if at all possible
for any disruption of your land
that i may bring
i am the human spirit

my mission is to wait here
to remember
i am only waiting
and one day
will leave

we are of the same God
i miss God
and you probably miss
Him too

i can see that you wait for God
to take me away from you

as much as i wait
to be taken
i am only welcome here
because of God and
you and i must
submit

we both call out as one voice, reminding ourselves and
God that
   — i am not of you; i am only passing through.

    2.

earth does not want us here
and maybe we do not really want to be here either
is it that we are waiting to be taken
and that when it happens man and earth
can be at peace?

till then may we not destroy earth while we wait.

Nature and I

circle and crowd in
that is the creed of the pack

attack! and take
your share of the meat

tear and rip the trapped soul
till you get to the heart

    and then, what?

harsh words to be sure
that describe nature's way of feeding

but though we might look away
there is no crime or sin
only instinct for catching one's prey

    so now what?

we act as nature
but we are not like her
for the same act
in us is cruelty

on a summer night i feel a breeze
and am soothed by the sound
of the birds by the water
and beyond that —
out of reach
out of sight
out of ear

in the woods beyond coyotes
tearing a rabbit to bits
        — what of it?

it is nature not us
we have laws and so does nature

odd that i am led
to a thought to wonder if
we belong here at all
for we are not like her
try as we might
to fit in

in the end
i can only say
i am only here for a while
        — i am not of her; i am only passing through.

Part Two:
Voices Not My Own

It Is So Quiet

I know a man who worked at a fire station watch tower. He searched daily for fires in the forest at the top of the watch tower. He told me once, "It is so quiet up here, at times I can hear my blood moving through my veins, and I hear my voice talking to me . . . which is different from when I am talking to myself.

He said, "It is so quiet that I can hear the silence."

Voices Not My Own (1)

i look inside myself and it is dark
i look outside myself and it is dark

i imagine i see images
coming in and going out

of windows doorways
portals and passages

hundreds of rooms in my soul
hundreds of guests making it home

i hear voices coming in
i hear voices going out

only one is my own
all the others are not

> look inside and most likely it is not all quiet
> there are voices inside us and we should
> be aware of them know them and learn
> what to do about them.

Voices Not My Own (2)

1.
when i wake
who shall i be
the same as i am now

   — i hope not

if in my sleep
the old self would die
when i wake
i would be someone new

   — then i could see God

though it never comes to pass
it is the only hope i have to help me sleep
— the belief that i will wake up new

if this hope dies
i will follow

   — and soon.

2.
this voice is not my own
— i recorded it as i heard it

how do we live
without hope
though i breathe do i live
is life more than breath

without hope
though i breathe
life itself is not enough
without hope
what power has hope in our life

in the midst of failure even when
hope is not a reality hope
still remains for me
to lean on it.

Voices Not My Own (3)

i am usually lonely
as i believe all people are
it is a battle
whether we give in
or imagine a win
     —a battle no one else sees

the deafening roar of silence
wears my soul
where is my consoler
if it is in a small still voice
then show yourself
if not
i must pretend you are there
     —to stay alive i must imagine victory

i wake to my usual dark room
in the early morning
the eerie quietness
reminds me again
of the voices i hear
in my sleep
voices not my own
     —crying out for someone to hear
     looking for a spiritual priest
inside me.

A Puzzle and a Reality

when i laugh or cry
it feels as if something inside wants out
and something else wants in

being alone with my thoughts is a silent pain
being alone means there is no one
with whom to share

who would want me like this?

Jesus, the Man

Did Jesus, the man, hear a voice — a voice not his own:
"I cannot come Myself so I send you; I cannot be a
sacrifice Myself so I send you in my stead."

Did Jesus, the man, follow a voice, a voice not his own:
"I speak of a truth through you, a truth that will
pierce every soul; either they will follow you or seek
to kill you, but either way the truth remains the
same."

Jesus, the man, heard a voice, a voice not his own:
and died an unspeakable death with a message so
pure that it could open any heart without the need of
buildings or the doctrines of men.

Why do we insist a life to be sacrificed before we were
willing to listen?

Powerful words are like a wind that fans our hearts
We only have to listen to feel the fire within

Whether it be of God or us
we would be wise to listen.

What Is This Voice I Hear

i am in a mad rush
to become what i want to become
and i know not how

what is this voice i hear inside
that has led me
to take what i have not earned
and caused me to believe
it is my right to have it

all the world bows
to what it cannot have
so gradually and yet so suddenly
the world is snuffed out

selfishness seeks to reap the desirable things of life
without sowing into them

selfishness wants not to reap the consequences
of the evil it sows into life.

In Silence I Contemplate

1.

in silence i contemplate
and observe others from a distance
i imagine i can love without getting close

then if i stumble
no one will get a good look
no one will know

i am safe by keeping my distance
therefore the risk of love is not risked
my fear of love my safety.

2.

i heard this voice rise up from my soul
i knew it was not my own
what voice speaks wanting to share its
fear of life and love

— without the willingness to risk love
fear is like a stagnant pond without water flowing
through it

how many drinks can you take from the pond
before it poisons you?

i did not see myself as the one in need of this message
— maybe i will need it later.

If I Could Reach Inside My Soul

how can i reach into my soul
let you feel what it feels
show you what it knows

there's a fight going on
i need your hand
i need your smile
just hold me for a while

how can i reach into my soul
take out the rage
take out the despair

there's a fight going on
i need your hand
i need your smile
just hold me for a while

how can i reach into my soul
and fill it with rest and solitude
so peace can reign there

there's a fight going on
i need your hand
i need your smile
just hold me for a while

till i find the strength to reach inside
will you hold me will you love me
soothe my fear

there's a fight going on
i need your hand
i need your smile
just hold me for a while.

Innocence Rebuffed

A young boy shyly approached the towering rough-looking man casting a huge shadow in the morning sun. The boy had been watching all morning as the bulldozer the man was driving scraped the wildflowers and grass from a meadow.

It was the talk of the small town, how a new subdivision was going in where the old meadow had been—the old meadow where the kids had played for generations.

The young boy waited as the man climbed down from the bulldozer for a drink of cold water and then eagerly put forth this question, "Why do you hate it? The meadow, I mean. Do you hate the flowers, too, or just the meadow?"

The man said, "Grow up," and walked away.

Puzzled, the boy said to the man's back, "I think it is because you are greedy."

Suddenly, the young boy's mother called out, and he ran home. And somehow he knew that his comments to the bulldozing man were of a voice not his own.

These Walls Are Crumbling

these walls are crumbling in
the light is going out
the flower in the vase is wilting
i see no hope for living

the sun brings the dawn
i am rested now
all plans seem new
maybe i will not give up.

A Thought on Suicide

Do not be fooled: they who want to — will.

1.

i am not me
therefore whoever
is me needs to die
then i can rest
when they are gone

i see the quietness of the dawn
no one is speaking
the only sound is of nature waking
the noise inside me
whispering my last thoughts

may i be a lesson for all who need answers
—if there is no one who can help you
they cannot condemn you.

2.

beyond my mind
beyond my heart
lies the controller
it is absolute
no matter
who
wants
to help

stand in line
wait till i

convince you
there is no help

then take the shovel and
bury the evidence
be sure you
get paid for all
the effort.

    3.

now
ask the question
whose side are you on yours or mine
— best wait till morning to decide.

There Are Movements I See

1.
there are movements
—a quick shadow streaking
        past my side
what is it i see?

—a thought passing
        through me
too quick to read

there are movements
—clouds growing dark mean
        rain for the farmer
what is it i see?
—a squirrel running for cover
        safety in the trees

there are movements
—a clock that owns me
        time rushes on
where will i be next year at this time?
—these movements inside me
        outside me
make me want to be fearless
not run for cover
        or is the squirrel smarter than i?

2.
like dark clouds before the rain
my thoughts pursue me
        i cannot run for cover
—so i am caught
in the sudden downpour of my thoughts

i sit inside and watch the rain come down
i am on the constant run for more income
— and these questions plague me
    will i make it intact till my death?
    will i ever enjoy my rest?
    why would God care about me
    when others' lives are more despairing?
i only suffer as a wandering soul
too obsessed to be thankful
for all the goods i have

worst of all
time is measured by a clock
— and the clock has no heart

if days were slower it would only be worse
if days were faster it would only be worse
if days were fuller it would only be worse
if days were emptier it would only be worse
— waiting on hope has done me in

where then is the hidden meaning to life?
where is the place of all healing?
does the sound of time ticking make us deaf
to hearing Your voice speaking to our insides?

i question my christian roots
there are as many christians lost as any found
we are so dishonest
and i fear that will never change

is the unspoken christian creed
to appear as if nothing is bothering us and so take the
attitude of prayer as if appearances will save us?

3.

there are movements
— deep within my soul
    i know i am not the owner of me
— my thoughts battle with these thoughts
what is in my soul must come out
    i can only hope that my voice is like the voice
i imagine it could be.

The Cry of Her Children

The mother walked past the room
where her daughter lay sleeping
She paused, as if knowing a secret pain existed there
She waited, listening to her daughter's quiet breathing
A mother can always hear the cry of her children,
even as they sleep

> *a voice only a mother can hear*
> *not audible to the ear*
> *— a different kind of hearing.*

Alone with My Thoughts

alone with my thoughts
contemplating in silence
is this imagined or is it real?

a knocking at my soul
a door swinging both ways

voices coming in
voices going out

i need a guard who knows me
a guard i can trust

who knows when to open the door
and when to close it?

the hollow whispers are haunting me
the hinges on my door are broken

the fear of knowing my house
has been invaded by strangers

and knowing they will not leave
without a fight

the fear of not knowing what to do
brings me to my knees to plead

alone with my thoughts
contemplating in silence
is this imagined or is it real?

is the power i seek the power
that can guard my soul
and bring me peace?

i have given my allegiance
to the power i seek
and i seek to worship
and serve this power

now may He make Himself known this hour

for i am a living soul
in need of a Godly presence
to comfort my spirit
and guard my house.

I Am Mostly Lonely at Night
(a poem of addiction)

cool morning air
wash my tears
ease the memory
of last night

first peek of sun
still my soul
breathe into me
new air

noise of morning
sounds of waking
may i be the first
in my universe
to break the silence
before the cricket sleeps

erase the memory
of my hands
reaching out
remembering nothing

the pain of not knowing
if something
happened or did not
happen

as i wake
the cool morning air
washes my tears
erasing the memory

of all the nights
as the sounds of the morning fade
the day begins to stir
may i have breath
enough to endure

for the nights yet to come
are lived by some foe
deep inside my
soul.

For the Love of Strangers

we give up half our income to pay
to sit outside in the heat and cold
on hard benches crowded up against
each other
to be entertained
we sit in smoky rooms with loud music
leaning or slouching in iron chairs
wanting to be noticed
staying out late
with too little rest

it would not be the same if no one else came
we do it all *for the love of strangers*

an unknown crave
a need beyond us
a hidden confession
a desire not met
to be admired by others
to be amongst them
to watch them
to be watched by them
to dance together
to cheer together
to watch the show
or sit in a busy mall
to satisfy an inside crave
it would not be the same if no one else came
we do it all *for the love of strangers*

the morning comes
we wait till the emptiness fills us

we must go again
never to be satisfied
not inhibited not judged
what void does it answer
to be amongst strangers
on a crowded street
to be ourselves with all to witness
it would not be the same if no one else came
we do it all *for the love of strangers.*

My Love Has Gone to the Dogs

i was pretty
i was noticed
i married three times

i am sixty-nine
i am alone
and you ask me
why i have four dogs

they hear my soul cry
they notice me
and i am loved

my love has gone to the dogs.

Part Three:
Portals and Passages

The Fog

see how the fog moves through the forest
it causes us to pause
and notice the beauty of it all
we are stilled and we are moved
and better for it

see how the fog moves through the forest
we are overcome by the possibility of mystery
to know what we do not know
and are excited with fright

see how the fog moves through the forest
will we ever get back if we enter
will it be safe
do i have what it takes
the fog moves through the forest
it is only for a while then lifts
but while it lasts i seek its truth inside and out

see how the fog moves through the forest
it is as You desire
and it moves us as You desire
You created it all
You make us pause to notice
what we need to know
gracious to accept our attempt at humility.

I Woke Up Early

1.
i woke up early
three a.m.
i heard a voice
inside me
i heard my spirit speak

how do i know this?

because we both wept for joy
a joy unknown till that moment

what does that prove?

it may not prove a thing
until you have experienced it.

2.
maybe you will never hear your spirit speak to you
maybe you will never have a conversation with your spirit
maybe you will never know
maybe someday
maybe never

the proof is in the hearing

i woke up early
three a.m.
i heard a voice
inside me
i heard my spirit speak.

Five Poems

1. *Is Prayer*

is prayer
the returning to the spiritual womb
and then going further in
to the place from whence we came

i see that image before me
as i contemplate the idea
of prayer

i go to a place i sense i know
it seems unreal in this life
yet it beckons me
to follow it

— or do i imagine —
that i come
to the place where i began
and the remembrance of all things
appears to be within reach.

2. *In My Sleep*

in my sleep i have these conversations
— all night it seems —
with some other being
who speaks to me such apparent revelations of truth
i must debate and reason with it
whether the information is of value
or not

this has been going on for some time
i have been aware of it for some time
when i share it with others a blank look on their faces

tells me that at best they believe that i believe
yet still it is unbelievable to them
— that which to me is a profound reality
and something i must reckon with —

    3. The Calling
a depression haunts me if i choose to ignore
       the rumble of this voice

the voice will not rest until it delivers the message
       "do not wait, go now"

i am puzzled for it sounds like the daily horoscope
       yet somehow i am supposed to discern the meaning

it is like so many testimonies of voices i hear
       where the interpretations remain ambiguous

there is conflict of knowing which voices i should listen to
       and which ones are only passing through

not every voice is to be heeded
       and our attempts to discern meaning fail more often
       than not

is the lesson here that we are vulnerable
that we need a God who does not require us to seek the
truth through unknown voices?

4. More Questions

what is a question but a premonition of something
more to know?
do the questions bring us closer to a truth?
if so, then does this poem helps broaden the under-
standing of premonitions?

any more questions?

5. The Peace

may i find peace
with the life i have been dealt
and the way i am to live it

some of us have choices
and some of us do not
may i find peace
with the life i have
been dealt.

Contemplation and Dreams

1.

a dream passed by my soul last night
i think my spirit invited it in
or did it enter without invitation
whichever — my memory is faint
though i am fairly sure
the spirit of the sender did visit

my concerns are
was the spirit sending out a plea for help
or a desire for something more
or was it a weary traveler in need of a place to rest
or a thief out to steal
— whichever
i knew of its presence

the discernment is
the visitor in my dream last night was different
from other hosts that have entered my soul
with a mission or a message
and it was different from the times
when other powers pursued spirits on the run
when the spirits needed a place to hide and would knock
at my door

the truth is
my soul is as a house mostly unguarded
any can enter and my dreams are as a doorway
so if they find my house appealing
they may choose to stay
but if so i may have a fight on my hands
or be tormented or enslaved

or they may mean no harm
    —if they are only passing through.

    2a.
i now know when my door has been opened
and my house has been visited
or if the visitors have not left

dreams are the clues that spirits have traveled
through the soul
if the soul is the house of our spirits
and if our spirits are its guards
then do we guard well
—and if not how do we learn to guard

can we visit other souls through our dreams and visions
do our prayers send out our messages
can we guide the messages to the intended destination
can other identities pick up these messages
what should i do when a passing spirit visits
can we be sure of the visit
depend on our sense of it as a truth

do spirits travel from our body
or do they only send their voices
do the dead send their spirits to roam
do the living only send the voice of their spirits
is that prayer or not

do we have a host of other principalities and powers
traveling this realm with access to our soul
how can we guard ourselves
how can we learn

is this reality or
am i a victim of my imagination
can i tell the difference between imagination and reality
am i delusional
the poetry fantasy
if so does it still hold some truth worth exploring
true or not i am unsure
but you will find me there.

    2b.

jesus
if a messiah shows me this reality
arouses me and awakens my spirit
may i guard my soul and know
who is welcome and who is not

if your promises be true
and the spirit of God inhabits my soul
watches after me
lights my way to this understanding
so that my prayers reach a safe destination
may my soul find rest
in you and others like you
and may i have a well-guarded and strong spirit

is this part of the mission of a messiah
—the one who shows us and teaches us—
so we can know what to do
so we can know how to see a dream
to discern other voices and all other realms
to know whether we are bound or free.

3.

the heavens are contacting us
all the spirits of earth calling out
as we sleep and our dreams inviting them in

are our dreams the clues that the spirits
whether of the earth or heaven
are on the loose
do they come calling when the body sleeps
to what spirits are our souls bound or in allegiance

arise o spirit of mine and find peace so my soul can rest
i am in need of a messiah — whether jesus or another
are they all the same?

Dreams Concerning the Future

one night while i slept
i dreamed of a future event
that eventually happened
i cataloged this with the other ones

my question:
did it happen yesterday — before i dreamed it
or today — when I dreamed it
or will it be tomorrow — when the dream will come true.

In a Dream One Afternoon

In my dream —
I am far ahead of the group in my walk
I become afraid and sit down to wait
As I sit I contemplate a personal issue
and from out of nowhere I hear a voice say
"I have sent you ahead; wait there till I come and wait for
the others. You will be sent ahead always — learn how to
wait."

I suddenly awake from this dream
Lying on the sofa on a Sunday afternoon
the world seems different.

Invited In (1)

testimony one
    the great Spirit lives

    i hear the voice

    i have been invited

    i am going in.

testimony two
    though the condemned
    cannot walk in the
    light
    and the sick are not
    healed
    and the oppressed are not
    free

— the content and the happy
believe they already have Him
but they may not have Him

those who are known by God are known
because of His call not *their* call

without the grace and mercy of God
i would be unable to accept anything of value

His voice is not the same for all
    seek Me and you will find in Me
    the voice you seek

and each of us shall have a different testimony
as to how we believe God answers our prayers.

testimony three
> whatever is going to happen to me
> will happen to me and when it does
> my response to it is my strength
> and my strength is my response to life

> —God's gift to me is my strength to
> respond to whatever life gives

testimony four
> the great Spirit lives
> i hear the voice
> i have been invited in
> i am going in

> *i would prefer to know mercy awaits me*
> *rather than to expect answered prayers and miracles.*

Invited In (2) (conversation with self)

1.
is the noise i hear inside me fear
    that speaks to me like an anger
        with enemies?

like the food that feeds an inner war
    with an appetite to strike
        in need of enemies

    is war our way of fighting our fear?
    though i long for the place of rest
    i fear i will not have it in this life

    if my fear could be tamed and i had no anger
    it does not mean my neighbor will experience
        the same

    i am deluded to believe that if i am at peace with
        my fears
    it will also produce peace in the fears of
        my neighbor.

2.
there is a restlessness in me which is also fear
    a fear that leads me to ask whether
        God is for me or my enemy

i tumble headlong onto that unknown path
    where my fear cries in want of a God who cares
        about us all and does not make us enemies

will my fear show me the way
to be at peace with the silence of God?
if fear is my path to God
does my fear have the courage to seek Him?

if God be not a caring God
then can i learn to love the God i fear
or am i to love that which i fear most?

will that love lead me to an inner peace
despite my fear of God?
why do we insist our enemies also be God's?

if God has no human enemies
then do i fight against God?
if i cannot save them and i cannot fight them
then is there peace in my fear in learning
to accept the differences between myself and my enemies
without need to destroy them?

— and how do i teach my children this lesson?

3.
if i am led to God
if i have an inner peace
will i fear my neighbor still?
shall i take up arms against my neighbor
if he considers me an enemy?
will God give me an inner peace
though i am called to war against my neighbor?

what is the meaning of "love my enemy"
when i war with him also?

or is the only way to love my enemy not to fight
to allow him to destroy my house?
i fear that kind of love most of all

and then i fear a self-righteous love
whereby i war because i am just and he is not

if all fear leads to war and
all of us are born to such fears
then i must come to terms with it

if God birthed in us such fears
then is it God's will that we come
to terms with it

can we learn peace in fear?
i think if we were patient in those
times of conflict a better discernment
might lead us to peace.

i hear "the fear of God is the beginning of wisdom"

it seems that most of us will fight and hope
for the best and risk it all on an unsolved theology.

4.
i wake suddenly from my dream
and attempt to write the words in a notebook
on the nightstand
the scenario is a familiar one

where do these words come from and why?
are the dreams only impressions of the day?

is it only my mind reasoning out these
    impressions while i sleep
or are the dreams from another source?
of this truth i am unsure
however these conversations in my sleep are
    all too familiar.

    5.
i thought it was not that unusual
to have conversations while sleeping
but years of sharing with friends have made
    me think otherwise
their responses revealing that they think i am
    from another planet.

Invited In (3)

1.
spirit of the knowing God

enter into me

— if only i would live to serve you

knock at the door of my soul

commune with my spirit

— dwell in me even if i am dull in every way.

2.
dark shadows at the entrance of my door

seek my will

— to have my will is to have me

spirit of the knowing God

protect me from the shadows

— return your memory to me

the memory i had of You before my birth.

3.

living God breathe upon me

i shall become a living soul

and my heart mind body and spirit

will have life.

As the Breeze

as the breeze comes naturally
and goes where it will
so is my belief in You
without borders

You are before the beginning
and beyond the end
without definition

You are my rest

therefore i judge no one
for enjoying the breeze
and being part of it

judge me not for the same

which one of us can control the wind?
it moves as it was made to move
and we are at its mercy

or is there another way to God?

so why build walls to protect us
from the breeze
and then wonder why
at our disbelief

as if the walls were the proof God is here?

Confession from Her and Him

1.

her confession to God and her lover

i want from God what you cannot give
i want from you what God cannot give

his confession to God and his lover

i want from God what He can give
i want from you what you can give.

2.

the words came in a dream
like a revelation that we should know
yet one that remains hidden
like an unknown confession inside us
waiting to be discovered.

Take on Quantum Physics Version Two

1.
—nothing is as it seems

—we are as special as we want to believe
it is within our being to want to believe it so

—if the makeup of all things is so dynamic
intricate and so well designed
then what need would God have for a bible
if there is a God and He needs a bible for us
then we are the dilemma of the universe

—the imagination of man is nothing compared to this

—how can we be in sin if all the other parts of the universe
have no sin?

—if all the particles of all beings are related then how is it
possible we are a glitch?

—what is the inert in us that seeks to be a unique offering
to the universe?
we conceive of gods and then seek their instruction
lift ourselves up as special to the gods we have conceived
create in ourselves a position of needing forgiveness

—how does quantum physics fit into that nature?
—is nothing as it seems?
—is God greater than we thought?
—greater than our belief of how God is

if quantum physics is so then God made quantum physics so.

2.

what we don't see is as real as what we do see
is the meaning of faith to move what is unseen into the
seen?
did Christ know this but not know how to teach us?
is all possible knowledge to be had in that teaching?
if so, we need to seek that truth in all things

does everything exist now — the past present and future?
what teaching can explain it to us in a way that we can
grasp?
do we only die to this reality and move on to the next?
how does the human existence compare to all other
existences?
do the answers to these questions lead to more questions
that lead to answers with more questions?

this mystery gives me more confirmation to live closer to
my heart
and to believe more in the thought that we are not alone as
humans
that possibly we are in a crowded universe with many
other beings and entities

quantum physics is a vital part of the understanding that
nothing is as it seems and that God is greater than we thought.

3.

all things are possible to he who believes
say to the mountain, "be cast into the sea"
and it will be done

is quantum physics a look into the truth of this saying
where the possible becomes probable
where the impossible becomes possible

where the unimagined becomes imagined
where discovery is a joy of the truth
and nothing is at it seems?

— meaning that if faith is a part of quantum physics
then it is the part that can cast mountains into seas

is quantum physics a look into the portals and passages of all
realms?
does the universe have a soul and a spirit?
does the earth also have a soul and a spirit?

did God create the soul of the universe and give it a spirit
and say to it "live"?

    4.
to hear the sounds around you better
simply close your eyes

technology is our invention
because it works it is His creation

technology can lead us away
from the most valuable truths
or it can lead us into
the most valuable
truths.

    5.
being that quantum physics is
— to ignore it is like a wishful thinker who does not
grapple with truth
but only takes what agrees with him and only
believes what agrees with his truth.

The Story of Aspens

One afternoon I hiked a high mountain trail, where the aspens grow. After about two hours on the trail, just before I peaked the top of a crest, I saw a woman sitting on a rock at the edge, just a few yards off the trail. She was weeping and the sound of her sobs mixed with the roar of the river below startled my quiet, contemplative stride. I stopped and paused for a moment before I decided to approach her. I was not sure my decision was the right one, but it didn't seem right to pass on by. My heart pounded as I quietly walked up behind her to gently tap her on the shoulder. As she turned to me I asked nervously but courteously the reason for her tears and if I could be of any help.

The woman did not seem startled at my sudden appearance, which surprised me. She replied that she had heard a voice inside, and pointed to her heart. "The voice tells me, 'I am the aspens and I know your name. We know everyone's name.' " The woman then added that another voice had also spoken to her, saying, "'We are the rivers that collect the tears of the great Spirit, for all the living of the earth drink of the tears.'" And she then said, "And so I weep."

I was stunned at her reply and perplexed as to how to respond. The words she spoke seemed to make sense to her, but I was caught off guard at the sudden descriptive nature of aspens and rivers and a great Spirit. Often I find we share a belief, not understanding that the words do not mean the same to the listener as they do to us. Had she read some book, cultivated some belief? Why was she expressing what she believed?

I decided to listen, not knowing what would come next. I reminded myself that I had stopped to help and that now I was committed to follow through. But no answer came to mind. Instead I acknowledged her reply by nodding my head, as if I understood, then I asked again if there was anything I could do for her.

She looked at me, clearly puzzled, then spoke again about the aspens and the rivers. Without realizing how I got there, I was soon sitting a few feet from her below the rock where she sat. She expounded on how the aspen trees lose their leaves, while other trees in the mountains keep theirs. "It is a show for us," she said, "to see that they, the aspens, suffer in the winter without complaint, while the other trees in the mountains keep their leaves. It is the aspens, don't you see, that shine in color and attract the interest of the people and complain not, even though in a few weeks they will be without the warmth of their leaves."

Then she continued, "The aspens do not complain, for they accept the will of the great Spirit. Because I have suffered much these past years myself, I know it is the aspens who know my despair, for they suffer also. Now they comfort me, and they assure me that I will be comforted again and enjoy better seasons."

She turned to me. "Can you hear their song as their leaves move in the autumn wind? I can hear them speaking; their song soothes my pain."

I could not imagine what kind of grief she was now experiencing and what events had brought her here to this mountain trail. A sudden thought flashed through my mind: had she come to these realizations as she was sitting here? Surely that was possible, that now she was sharing them as new thoughts, born but as yet undefined. But though the words were abstract and disconcerting to me, penetrating in a haunting kind of way.

At this point there were a few moments of silence. Finally I spoke. "And the rivers, what do they say?"

More silence, as if she had not heard me. Then, "The rivers provide us with the essence of life, or the tears of the great Spirit. The rain is the tears of God, and it replenishes and nourishes the earth. Tears are both joy and pain. The lesson is that life is both joy and pain, and now my tears are the testimony of that lesson, and the nourishment of my tears helps bring me joy, and helps comfort my pain. For God is of joy and pain. If you will listen as I have, then you will also know as you drink from the waters of heaven, which are now in these rivers below, you can be reminded of the tears of the great Spirit and know that your own tears are created in you to know yourself, and to know the great Spirit who has created the tears for you."

At this point I had stopped wanting to comprehend her statements. In fact, I wanted to leave as quickly as possible. In my confusion I heard the roar of the river, which now seemed more distinct, and the wind, which seemed so strong, blowing through the aspens. The woman's seemingly peaceful voice frightened me, but how could I back out of this situation politely? Then, as I was about to stand up and take my leave, a voice inside me began to whisper the revelation of these two elements of the mountains. I began to see a place inside myself, a place that needed to hear this strange woman's strange words.

My movements after that remain somewhat vague in my memory, as if I were moving outside myself. Suddenly I felt I had to close my eyes for a moment. As I did, I saw the woman at the edge of the crest, who had turned from me and was now weeping again. I heard her crying, and then I was crying uncontrollably as well.

Suddenly I became ashamed, for I imagined that she would see me crying, a stranger who had stopped to help her but who was weak and now crying at her side.

I wanted to be away from there, continue my hike. Why had I stopped? As these thoughts raced through my head, a warm kiss on my forehead just above my eyes took my breath away. I quickly opened them to see what was happening.

But the woman was gone.

I stumbled to my feet, breathing heavily. How had she left so quickly after the kiss that I had not been able to see which way she had gone? But then a more disturbing thought entered my mind. What if she had never been there at all, if I had imagined everything? Slowly I arose and moved closer to the edge of the crest. Truth be told, I wondered if she could have jumped. Perhaps her rambling poetic thoughts were her last desperate grasp on life. But I did not want to believe it. On the other hand, I had no real answer otherwise.

It was as if I were waking from a dream. I slowly guided my thoughts back to my own reality. For a few moments I felt myself flooded with a warmth and a peace. I liked the feeling, but did not understand it. I decided not stay at that place any longer, and resumed my hike, dazed, yet at peace. When I glanced at my watch I saw that the whole event had taken only about twenty minutes. Was it real? I never learned the answer to that question.

One more incident occurred as I began to descend the trail. A young couple spotted me as I was stepping down from the rock at the edge of the crest. Still delirious from the woman's quick disappearance, I was not feeling altogether myself, and for some reason the young couple were interested in me and innocently asked if I were alone. They suggested that if I were, it must be lonely to be way up here without a companion to keep me company. I begged to differ, stating assuredly that I was not lonely, for I had a magnificent view from the rock beside the oak tree on that ledge. "Like the oak," I said, "I came here for the view and to feel the wind. The oak is not lonely, for all the forest keeps it company; the squirrels and other animals feast from its fruit and eagles rest upon its branches."

As I said these words, I recognized the were not my own. But whose were they? They had been formed by years of experience, but not my experience; yet they had come rolling from my lips. The young couple was quiet and gracious. They acknowledged my statement and then continued their walk, passing by me on the trail. The young man looked back at me once, as if to get a bearing on my reply. I do not know what their conversation was on the trail, or if they comprehended what I said or if I made any sense at all. But if the woman was only a figment of my imagination, then perhaps they were as well.

And what did that say about me?

The Aspen The Rivers The Oak

1. the aspen
the lady of ghosts sits on the high cliffs
she recites the words of understanding
for any who have ears to hear and eyes to see
it is no wonder she sits alone

today she sings the song of the aspen
the tree that sheds its leaves
when others keep theirs for the winter
who knows the why of it

the lady of ghosts knows and sings her song
to those who suffer the days without relief
for who else knows the melody of comfort
of the aspen tree's fate

lay me bare and then watch over me
for the cold needs Your warm breath
the days will pass as i look
for Your smile and warmth
come spring i will bear leaves again

how shall i know you my Lord
lest i am willing at Your hands to be stripped
and clothed at Your will
the lesson for all who suffer
must be to come to You for comfort

though the winter hurts my limbs
and the wind pierces my wooden soul
it is only You who comfort me and make me a show
for others to learn what it is to lean on You
i am the lady of ghosts

singing the song of the aspen
though i am naked in winter
i am clothed eternally with Your comfort
and suffer for those who are in need of You.

    2. *the rivers*
may the tears of God
rain on me
may i drink from the rivers they fill

i walk the meadows and the hills
and thirst knowing not what i thirst for
lest it be to be filled by You

i cry tears of joy and tears of sorrow
each day has enough for us
to walk in its length and breadth

prepare us for tomorrow
how is it we learn not to weep
to hold back till at last
like a flood it destroys
any fertile land that might have been

it is the wise who weep often
and water the fields for growth
who see the tears of god
have filled their own.

    3. *the oak*
the oak said i am not lonely
the view makes all the difference
see my limbs and how the eagles find rest
and the acorns at my feet are the fruit
for the squirrels and other animals.

The God I Know

1.
the god i know
is the god i trust

each morning comes
as it has for thousands of years

my soul is at peace
and my spirit is fed

i am a seeker of the inner self
the place where i believe truths are found

come and seek for yourself
the time it takes is well spent
the effort put forth is well rewarded.

2.
there is no end
to the inner self
only more

eyes to see
ears to hear
look within
for living
waters.

3.

to me —
the reality of the realms of life
is as a rainy day
the rain may come as a flood
or a gentle pour
some of us are caught in tragedies
without justice
and others live lives without
real trial or test

what do i make of it but to seek and hope to find
whether there is a fairness and equality to it all

my aching soul seeks to be satisfied
it wants to know that the god i seek
will make it right for all souls.

Part Four:
Way of Life

Shadow of a Cross Made by Men

I shed the shadow of the Crosses built by the hands of men
    for their names are carved on these Crosses
    made of wood

I hold onto the Cross that is in my heart
    where the names of men are not worshiped

Their shadow will never again dictate my belief
    or my way of life
    and I pray I will never again seek their Crosses
    as my guide

May I be true to the God that dwells in my heart
    mind and soul

      amen.

The Wheat and Chaff

When others esteem their own doctrines as the only way to truth, they become like chaff in a wheat field

There is no nourishment in the chaff

Bread is not made from chaff

Bread is made from wheat

> *may I learn how to separate the chaff from the wheat in my own heart and blame not others if I fail to do so.*

The Day the Earth Ended

1.
the day the earth ended
was the day heaven began

and we fought it till the end

amen.

2.
if hell is under the earth
and heaven is above the earth

if earth is revolving around the sun with other planets in a
solar system that makes up part of a galaxy that is a part of
the universe

then we need to have a better look at the whole concept
see where to look for the God who is the maker of it all

amen.

3.
once upon a time i charted a course for my life
soon i discovered the road was not as the map said
so i traveled the course the best i could
as i look back it seems some of us are luckier than others

i can see there are many beliefs that offer different
explanations from mine
concerning the road we all have to travel i can only hope
our differences do not cause too much offense

amen.

4.

every truth i have ever heard has been amended
several times
amended to suit the time the season the place
and the ones who have amended it

we treat truth like seasons ever changing
like the weather always unpredictable

maybe the definition of truth needs amending
but i think we fear to think of our scriptures as
amended

amen.

The Dream of a Hurting Lover

1.
I waited for you all day
believing you would come to me

I found out years later
that you waited for me to come to you

My love for you is like an invalid
waiting to be healed by your touch

The puzzle is that we both wait to see
who will rise first and knock at the other's door.

2.
Can I an invalid rise and go to my lover
though this be only a dream can dreams deliver

Can I dare to trust the dream and go
knock at the door only to be rejected

Is it of more value to rise and dare
or to wait and dare

My love has run and hid itself in the arms of my pride
for I cannot face the question

Do I knock first or wait
whichever I choose it is the answer I long for

I sense that whoever rises first and knocks
carries the healing with them

And healing might not always have
the answer we want.

When Trust Has Been Broken

1.
when trust has been broken
　　like a strong branch of oak

can it be repaired
　　or will a new one have to grow?

2.
i have heard my own voice and it speaks
　　that the peace i seek of lost friendship will take time
and a new branch will sprout

but for now i must allow time to produce
　　the courage and patience to trust again.

3.
if i am the only one i can trust
　　i doubt i will be able to live up to it.

4.
without wounds and healing
　　how else will the wrinkles of age show their beauty?

Two Leagues Ahead of the Sun

I knew a man who was two leagues ahead of the sun
"Slow down," he said, "or you will miss what God has
done."

I dreamed I saw a shadow once stall in the air
as if the wind saw the beauty and stopped to stare.

Move too fast and we miss it all
Move too slow and we all fall
What time is it now
    time to change –
    time to see –
    time to feel –
What's happening now?

I walked away from my day job to follow the dream
If I don't follow now . . . when?

What is in my soul must come out
It's about a truth I was told about

Move too fast and we miss it all
Move too slow and we all fall
What time is it now
    time to change –
    time to see –
    time to feel –
What's happening now?

The world is at a loss for what's at stake
and men seem determined to die or take

The living creed is already given
and we spin it like a yarn as if truth were ours to make.

Move too fast and we miss it all
Move too slow and we all fall
What time is it now
  time to change —
  time to see —
  time to feel —
What's happening now?

Till the morning sun comes and the evening sun rests
I will listen for the distant drum of the heavens
in the movement of the wind

Announcing the same message again and again saying,
"Without rest for your soul there is nothing else greater to
gain"

Move too fast and we miss it all
Move too slow and we all fall
What time is it now
  time to change —
  time to see —
  time to feel —
What's happening now?

Are We Not All God's Children

are we not all God's children
are we not all entitled to have joy in a truth
that we discover on our own?

are we not to be free to contemplate
on our own concerning a spiritual matter
even when it disagrees with the consensus of others?

My Compass, My Conscience

my conscience is like a compass to me
    it is my way to see my way

my God is the Maker of my compass
    the Maker of me

every birth comes with a compass
    every compass points to the Maker

every day is either lost or found
    every breath is a time to seek

there is life in us that must be stirred
    a life that must be born

our life is our witness
    whether our compass points to God

    or not.

Follow the God in Your Heart

whatever the risks
there is no assurance of our grab for truth
we grab and hope it is truth
then preach it to others
if we change our views
we preach that new version

if this be so and i think it is
then i will follow the God in my heart
and not bother to live according to this wind
that blows us every which way and then seeks company

the changes in life will be my own
my life in action will be my sermon
i do not want you to follow the winds of others
but to follow your own
i think maybe then God's mercy will take hold

*i do not seek converts of my own to validate the God in my soul
only validation that we all have the same freedom.*

Living Soul

if the soul is of the breath of God
if the soul was made to be the house of God
then it is a living house and a living soul

if the soul was made to be a place
where the spirit of God can dwell
if the soul is where our spirit dwells
then it is also the temple of God

if that is so then it is our temple
and the place we go to worship God

> *take my heart and my mind and my body*
> *mold and make me into the image of Your desire*
> *whatever You make of me is what i want to be*
>
> *make Yourself known to me so i can bow*
> *with knowledge and humility*
> *and have no excuse to bow to any other.*

If God

If God were human
> then our works would be glorious in His sight
> and our evil would cause Him to war against us

> *– it is a good thing God is not human*

If humans were as God
> then the heavens would be like the earth

If we are not good humans on earth
> then how can we be good Gods in heaven?

> *– it is a good thing humans are not Gods.*

My Own Peace

1.
i have my own peace
    even without answers

i have my own faith
    even without proof

i hear the quietness of the wilderness
    even with all its noise

i bow and i worship to the God in my heart
    because i am led there

    i am not seeking to sell you on the idea
    only confessing what i believe.

2.
if the same sense of God is not in you
    i have no argument with that

just because it is not in you
    is not evidence it does not exist

we separate at the path here
    i have my own peace and i will walk in it

may you also have your own peace and walk in it
    i wish you well

i am not seeking to make you a convert to my idea of peace
    only hope that you do not insist
    on making me a convert to yours

    this is a case when two beliefs disagree
    — one does not negate the other.

Who Made the Maker

1.
who made the maker?

    itself?

what is the sure bet?

    death?

what is love?

    human?

why the questions?

    ignorance?

why the questions?

    wisdom?

why the questions?

    free time?

2.
when is a good steak

    overdone?

The Cross I Bear

i am not sure of any messiahs
i have made my allegiance to a power better
i follow as i see Him lead

i owe no man my allegiance
but to treat him as an equal
it is the peace in which i walk
and the cross i bear.

The Red from the Sky

As the red from the sky cast its light upon
the water of the sea
I looked upon it and was blinded so that I could not see
the trail or the hill on which I stood
The light made everything dark before me
and as the distant sea reflected the light of the setting sun
I was awed by this common occurrence

A bird flies above where I stand
as if it is a part of a greater harmony
The bird needs not contemplate or be enlightened
by this harmony
as it is being what it was born to be
and takes to the air naturally

The moon is full tonight
its light permeating the sea below
I am entranced by the beauty of the scene
the shadows beyond the light haunting me
yet ministering to me simultaneously

The red from the sky fades as the dawn rises
Does the dawn ever seek to catch the sunset
and see if a mystery lies within
Does the dawn ever pause to glimpse a full moon longer
or watch the sea change colors
or view the birds in flight over the distant hill?

The dawn seems void of my emptiness and need.

There is a Fox

1.

i spy
you spy
i hide
you hide.

2.
i watch you
from out the window
as you come out for air.

3.
why have you chosen the juniper
bush in my front yard to live?
you have better choices
we are surrounded by hills
uninhabited by humans
so why my juniper bush?

4.

will i ever see the pups i hear
or will you take them away in the night?

is there harm in letting you stay
or is there harm in shooing you away?

5.
i have a fox pelt given to me by a friend
i assume you would be offended to know this
though i wish you no harm

but i also assume the same would be true for me
if you had a pelt of my species
i might find it hard to believe after seeing the pelt
that you meant me no harm.

Is There a Reason for Reason

Is there no end to reason?

I sat in the forest above a seasonal river. Just below a small swarm of bees hovered in the wildflowers in the meadow.

As I watched I imagined I heard this conversation:

What is my reason for living? one of the wildflowers was saying to one of the bees. *I am the reason you are living,* said the bee, *to give us life.*

The flower asked then, *What is your reason for living? To give the bears life,* said the bee.

And the wildflower asked, *And what is the bear's reason for living?*

The bee yelled then, as if in anger, *To take our honey!*

The wildflower was intimidated at the reply of the bee. It didn't seem right to me for the bees to be angry at the bears.

The conversation ended after that. It takes a human to get mad at bears for living.

Stay with Me

1.

the light in the sky is going down
the flame in my heart is glowing
stay with me

the look in your eyes
the poise of your silhouette against mine
is the love which stirs my soul
stay with me.

2.

i will never finish loving you
no one has taught me how
it came as naturally as the dawn
in the morning
stay with me.

3.

if we momentarily drift
may all the seasons of our love
be enough to catch us lest we fall
may we always court each other
knowing that we are the most precious part of our life.

4.

stay with me till the last moment of our breath
stay with me and forget not the first day
stay with me and i will wrap you in my arms
with the best i have to give.

5.

you walk with a beauty all your own
formed by the trials and hopes that are in you
my eyes my heart and my soul take you in
and knowing you will always be at my side
causes my love to grow

so after all is said and done
stay with me.

Without Question

1.

in the simplest of observations without agenda
the human form is a magnificent creation
a marvel of engineering genius
how it all works together to give life

it is also a mystery why a creator would make it
with so many flaws and operational failures
with such a short life as compared
to the universe and eternity

why would a perfect entity like God
create an imperfect being like us
then choose to dwell in us
as a part of our spirit?

at first thought we seem beautifully made
upon examination however i see we are flawed
that our whole concept of ourselves and God
is also flawed

a fear comes upon me
i realize it is time to rethink things
are we left here to survive by our own wit
— or is there the creativity wired in us
to make our survival as marvelous
— or as tragic as we want?

the questions of who we are why we are and what we are
— endless in our quest
our conclusions are speculative at best.

Part Five:
A Turn in the Road

And for What Purpose

1.
your church denominations are
like barbed wire to the open range

your doctrines are fencing us in
we are being separated from each other

and for what purpose?

2.
the way i see it
God made the open range

men made barbed wire fences and
that is the way it is and always will be

and for what purpose?

Beyond Us

could it be that
we are far from home
and our mission is
to live on earth
peaceably
while we
wait

wait
for the
return of
the ones who
brought us here
and have a purpose
for our being here

are they the ones we address as God?
are they the ones who gave us
the words we seek to live by?

my question is:
how many gods are there
and how many words are there to live by?

i am hoping
they will return and
that i have chosen the right god
whether i am alive or dead
if and when they come
i would like to know what the purpose of all this was

if there was one.

Rise Up

Rise up and go to the mountain top
so the eyes of our spirit can see
the One who lights the lamp of our soul
and who is the guardian of life

The God we seek is greater than
those who put a monetary price on God
with sermons meant to take from
what we have earned
to persuade us to believe we are closer to God
by supporting them

Only we can bring ourselves closer
— God requires not money; only people do

Do not dress your hearts in clothes or jewels
God gave us hearts to see with
not to clothe or adorn

We build churches to serve us
not for us to serve churches
Choose one
— the God in our heart or the god made by us

Rise up and go to the mountain top
so the eyes of our spirit can see
the One who lights the lamp of our soul
and who is the guardian of life

It is not what we wear or do not wear
It is not whether our hands are raised or folded
It is not our silence or our shouts
— It is with spirit and truth

Our life is the witness of our heart and soul
  No thing is as true a doctrine as
  "Do unto others as you would have done unto you."
  — Judged by it in every situation

Rise up and go to the mountain top
so the eyes of our spirit can see
the One who lights the lamp of our soul
and who is the guardian of life.

Saving Grace

1.
she grew up fast
with a lot to show for it

who could have told her
who would have known

evil follows beauty
quiet and sly as a fox

it takes its prey
while the owners sleep

they send the hounds out
all the noise and dirt flying

she liked to be admired
she liked to be watched

she wanted an easy way
who could have predicted this day

she disappeared without notice
except by a young boy selling papers
who saw her get in the van
willingly he said
and recognized her photo

now he is the hero
now she is shunned
her face distorted from the blow
where is her walk
where is her glow

the newspaper read *Saving Grace*
for that was her name

she feels betrayed
she says she will not heal

Saving Grace is now a phrase
she loathes and hates

the sermon on Sunday morning
causes her to stay away
we do not understand
for we were not beautiful once

and the words *Saving Grace*
have no memory for us
as they do her

will she heal in time
will the scent of fresh flowers return
or will she grow the more bitter

we cannot help her
so we ignore her.

2.
The old crippled man in the park says,
"Only time will tell if there will be a healing for Grace
till then may you find the mirror of your own soul
and see the tempter of the vanity in yourself

There is no difference between you and Grace
only she has come closer to truth for her trials
she walks a path of healing you know not of"

why should this man in a park
have the audacity to tell us things of life
as if he were wise and we were not?

"I have nothing to lose," he says,
"but by my honesty you do
I too have lost everything dear to me
I know what a lonely path healing can be."

The Living Ghost Towns

living ghost towns are like memories haunting
the truth in the people who once lived there

where life drags on with the numbness
because every day is the same
where romance is better imagined than lived
where fathers are better remembered dead than alive
where gusts of wind come without warning
where the stories of the "good times" are not
the stories lived

only when the last house is abandoned
will the last history be written
the ghosts are screaming at us *wanted dead or alive*
but we only settled in this town to survive

the ghosts whisper in our ears
it is time for you to go this is our town now
so when the last gas pump closes down
and boards replace windows
and the paint peels away
that is when the ghosts
are here to stay

it seems so sudden
though it was a long time coming
we did not believe it till it happened to us
the wind and insects are the only sounds now
when the quiet haunts us
when ghosts are about their business

we are taught not to listen to or believe
yet i see them everywhere

so how is it i am not to
believe in them

as i listen to the wind i swear i hear
the sound of their melodies
that haunt my soul.

The Mystery

We are the mystery for we continually accept ideas of God that fail us, but dare not change the ideas as if such a thing were forbidden.

We suffer loss all day long, then go to God with that loss, offer sacrifices of money, lifestyle, attitude, devotion, song, and worship.

We believe that God must love us in the way we think He should, that there is no other conceivable way it could be, even as we hoard goods for ourselves.

We are committed to warring with our neighbors concerning our differences of God, but feel not guilty for each of us sees our view of God as superior.

We complicate love with rules of guilt and we transgress rules as quickly as we make them.

Are we so blind and arrogant as to believe that God sees us as more special than any other creation?

We drink from the troughs of the spiritual with empty words, intoxicated by them, thinking if we keep coming and drinking that surely God will see our heart and give us what we want.

We learn the phrases of these individuals who to me are like wolves that trap us and eat our insides and take our goods for themselves.

We are dull and know it not.
We are dead and yet have breath in us still.
His words may be unburdened and light, but give us awhile and we will shackle ourselves and others.

We of This Democracy

we of this democracy of America
are unseeing to think
that all the world has the same dilemmas
unconsciously believing
we are more special than
anyone anywhere else

and that a democracy like ours
is the answer for the world from God
for us to distribute

> *maybe human rights is a better pursuit than democracy*
> *do I need a shield or can we discuss this possibility*
> *peacefully?*

We Are Not from Here

it seems we are not from here
though i believe we were created to be here
all the other creatures of earth live in harmony
we need a rule to guide us to show us how to get along
we need a golden rule

the animals do not

God made us to worship God as humans
God made animals to worship God as animals
we have a free will
animals are free
and have a will different from ours

we can only know animals
in the way we were made to know them
animals can only know us
in the way animals were made to know us
we can be friends in that way

animals do not cross over to be humans
though animal lovers might argue this
humans do not cross over to be animals
but perhaps our behavior would argue this

are animals more at home on earth than we are
it seems more their earth than ours
are we from somewhere else waiting to be taken
the scriptures in our books seem to believe it so

where do we go from here?

maybe looking to the gods is the answer
maybe to the content of religion and truth
maybe to the truth that will set us free
maybe that is the ultimate salvation

>some say the gods are inside us
>some say the gods are outside us
>maybe both or maybe neither
>but looking to god for answers
>is common to most humans

>as the animals know their home
>maybe we will someday know
>a place we can call home
>if the gods come and take us away

till then may we not be a burden to earth and the animals
when our time on earth is done
may we leave with as much dignity as possible
and remember the calamity we have caused
and as we wait for this God to come for us
may we determine to do a better job

i hope this God for whom we instinctively wait will forgive us
i hope salvation is not waiting for us to restore what we have
destroyed.

Why Do These Four Say the Same Thing

1.

the secret is simple
the way is clear
it is we who do not see it or hear it
there is no one belief that can save the world
no matter who follows us.

2.

at best
   – our life is only a dim light to guide us and others
   to warn others to follow their heart and not ours

   – to know that forgiveness is the best judgment of all

i must confess this
   – it seems forgiveness is easiest when i have the
   upper hand.

3.

my quiet tongue causes the tears to fall like rain
from my eyes
i am learning to trust the pain of a quiet tongue

its silence is like a heat that melts the cold snow
from my heart
i am comforted to know that silence has a voice too

as the snow melts from my heart it becomes a river of tears
and quietly waters the meadows of my soul

of all that i said or all that could have been said
it did not change your heart
and now i bear the pain of what i cannot change

can i trust the quietness of my tongue
for the many words i spoke helped no one

i now have only to trust my will to forgive you and me
to trust that forgiveness will bring the healing

so may my tears be like the snow that waters the earth
so new fruit can grow
may i learn to harvest it
and be nourished by the fruit of humility.

4.
metaphors are only descriptions of the real.

Love/Hate

1.
I wrote on a piece of paper all that I loved
    I contemplated
        and slowly completed the list on one page
        one page was sufficient

I wrote on a piece of paper all that I hated
    The words came out so quick and abundant
        that it filled several pages
        and I quit there although
        there was more, much more

Why is it we hate more than we love without trying?
    It comes naturally
        —now what?
        do we hide it
        or confess it?
Do I keep these pages or destroy them?

2.
Take my hand and never let me go
Hold me tight and hold me gentle P
lace your cheek next to mine
Our love will bring us smiles

While the day lasts
and the days turn into years
I will take you into my heart now and forever
to the place I have made for you and me.

3.

There is no rule to this prose
It seeks a place where the wildflowers grow
The sun gives us light and the trees give us shade
and the verse herein gives in to the instinct of my heart
my thought and my soul.

4.

So I practiced with much sensitivity
to allow more love in because it seems love needs
more practice than hate

practice practice practice.

Concerning a Friend

1.
when i needed a friend
    you were not there
you would not stand up for me
you would not take me on my word
you are a repeat of the same old stories
    told over and over again
    of betrayal.

2.
you were wrong not to believe me
you were wrong not to defend me
you did not see the truth of it at all

the friendship has taken a great fall
now i will keep you at a distance
    trusting you again
    will be as if it were from the beginning.

3.
i have given you no offense
    i was in need
the trust was not asking much
only that you give testimony of your
    trust in me
you had not that to give
no explanation as to why
you have let me down in the worst way

now i will keep a distance
between you and me.

4.

be not too close or familiar a friend
no matter how long a friend —
till it is tested it means little in fact bye-
      bye to the thought
      that it could be different.

5.

the earth is clay
the sky is air
the sun is heat

i observe it all
it is magnificent to me
it is a minister to me like no other
i will collect my thoughts and seek my peace
and look for a wisdom inside to guide me

again i will rise in the morning
look the day in the face
find a joy in life
and hopefully
find others to share it.

6.
A friend is a friend when he knows enough to give
when asked
      and not to question too much

if the friendship is not in the heart
then it will fail even before it is tested
a friend is a friend when he is willing to risk enough
to know how important it is to take one at his word.

7.
not to say it hasn't been good
i thought of you as the best of friends
　　— a brother

we have both lied to each other in our loyalty as friends
most likely it is the only lie we told each other

just because it ends doesn't mean all the miles before
were wasted
as they were some of the best miles i ever traveled

we are shallow dull and arrogant
now i know that the best friendships can end.

8.
there is always room for error

though i am willing to live with the loss
if ever we shall meet again i wonder
what the outcome will be

i will admit my own error
but i will not take yours or
be the only one to admit wrongdoing

as long as each of us owns up
there is room for the friendship
to renew itself

but till then
the sun will not stand still
and i will live it to the best

there is always room for error in my heart

i hope you have the same kind
of room in your heart
      for error

so if and till the time comes
      i will wait and see

      the end.

The Penjamo Bar, N. Hurley, New Mexico

1. The Penjamo Men

The "P" has fallen from the sign of the Penjamo Bar.

The men laugh and the owner laughs, "It is of no concern. We know where it is and we know what it is and that is all that matters."

They mean, of course, it is all that matters concerning the Penjamo Bar — good drinks, good laughs, good times, and good men.

> *We wash our memories clean.*
> *We are the men of Penjamo.*

The other men in the other town do not know true men. Though we fight amongst ourselves, we do not abandon each other. We are a people who fend for ourselves and we are a proud people.

The "P" is of no concern, for we will gather at the Penjamo Bar till it is no more. And maybe then we will still gather there to look at the stars, pass the beer, and be friends.

We are the men of Penjamo who live next to the tumbleweed and yucca and coyote and javelina, and desert dust and wild grass, with sunsets and sunrises as quiet as any, and with as many colors as anywhere.

We are free to live and breathe here; we are the men of Penjamo.

You will be served in our cantina
though we are not welcome in yours
Some say it is the tequila that gave us our name
but I think it's because we are from a place
where no one wants to come

The early barrio, it is our jewel, and we are happy with it, thank you.

So lean the "P" against the adobe wall; come in out of the noon sun and stay till the shade covers the door — or leave sooner or not.

2. The Penjamo Cross

The Penjamo Cross is a metal pole with a horizontal rod holding a sign of an arrow pointing to the Penjamo Bar door. It resembles a cross and nothing more.

No irreverence intended
Just an observation
And imagination.

(Since the writing of this poem the "P" has been put back on the sign.)

If They Could Talk of Hurley, New Mexico

a lone tree by the railroad station
both the station and the tree of an age
their bearing forgotten
yet no one in a hurry to end their life

the eyes of landmarks in rural towns of america
with tales of their own
secrets they keep to themselves
if they spoke, what would we hear
would our image of ourselves be the same

— or is it best not to ask?

All in All

all in all
i believe
we have
the freedom
to form our view
of life the way we see it

i am
in awe
mostly with
the unanswered
and the unknown
as it is greater than we are
and we are not allowed the knowledge of it

so
that being so
i have a freedom
to enjoy what life i have
to feel a continual nudge

to continue the seeking the way i do
i have no guilt in the truths not known to me
i have no guilt in not living the way some preach it
as if they do know

my hope is
that if any true wisdom
comes my way it will be with joy
for i seek the answers that will take us out of our cruelty
i believe we are a cruel people
maybe there are others who also seek answers of life

if so perhaps a light will shine from places
we have never seen

answers may come in ways we know not of
perhaps we need the freedom
to ask the questions and doubt those
who forbid us to ask and to seek a better truth.

Part Six:
Story Poems

How Green (1)

As the story goes, of two visitors one day in Hurley, NM...

A young couple made their way through the long dry flat plain of road on bicycles. Their gear and mountain bikes were well tuned and their muscles well toned. They were well educated to the degree that they knew what they believed and why ... or so they thought.

The hot air stung at their necks and throats as they pedaled on, seemingly without relief. Finally they came to a small town and looked around till they found shade and rested their eyes. Then they wandered up and down this small town till they spied two large smokestacks used for smelting copper. The young couple were disgusted at what they saw for they believed the smelter soot was everywhere.

They said to themselves, *Our mission is to help these poor people.* They sounded the alarm in the local cafe where a few regulars sat on stools at the counter and listened to the young couple who asked, *Do you not know the soot from the smokestacks is killing you?*

One man at a back table had been silent remembering how not having a smelter had also been killing them. Now he said, *Why is it that you and the bosses at the smelter are so concerned about us? Say what you came in to say and leave us, for we see life in the smelter, not death.*

Later that night the young couple approached another man on his roof. The man had a telescope and a map of the stars in his hand. He invited the young couple up on the roof and offered them cold beer. *Had they ever looked at the stars,* he asked.

The couple was angered by this man's question.

Why would you think we have never noticed the stars? they snapped. *Well,* the man said, *if you had, you would have soon seen that there is no way to count them.*

The young couple defensively rebuked the man and assured him they knew that. Then the man said he had been in this town a long time, working in the mine alongside his father, that his father had come there as a young man looking for work. The man explained, *the dust here may not be good for you, but we are used to it.*

We know what it has done to us, yet we cannot fully count the cost of life here, and neither can you count the cost if our living is taken away from us. We have raised our families here and we enjoy these quiet starry nights. So enjoy the evening with me for we believe friendship is better than the promise of your idea of a green earth.

He said, *just as we cannot count the stars neither can we count the cost of another man's life. Maybe in time after you have eaten our food and slept in our beds we can talk of this again. If you stay for the fall, winter, spring, and summer then, with God's help, you will have a vision of us, and then maybe you will not be so eager to save us.*

After a day's rest the young couple got on their bikes and headed west. They had not a mission anymore to help the people of Hurley, New Mexico.

I can only assume that each held to their view. The only difference is that the folks of Hurley were willing to accept the young couple as friends and the young couple were not willing to accept them — not unless they were the voice for the small town to the big corporations.

(I heard the story of this young couple from the man with the telescope. The man told me, "The odd thing is, the smoke stacks had not operated for years, but the young couple did not even take the time to notice. No one has ever asked us what we

want in the community; it seems we are the ones everyone uses
to further his own cause.")

How Green (2)

i stand tall
unbent by years
proud and silent
and a shadow of my former self
hardened by bosses

i am made of concrete and steel
i smell of sulfur till it suffocates the air around me
snow rain and wind hinder me not

i bring sadness and joy
the lives of many have leaned on me for support
i cry not for anyone's despair

i am the object of hope
like a holy article of faith in the church of life
for one small town i am the universe

a miracle happened during my peak
and a brother was born and he grew taller than i
and gave more hope to many

there were the nonbelievers
and skeptics in every crowd
who made many accusations against me
i stood against them and won

i can hear the drum roll now
though it brings no joy to my adversaries
as it was not their voices that brought this on
as the saying goes
the world does not stand still
and so the world decides my future

the news is out
i am coming down for good
no one can stop it

where do i go from here
    who am i?

(The smokestacks from the Phelps Dodge smelter in Hurley,
New Mexico, were imploded on June 5, 2007 at approximately
10:00 a.m. Of note is the fact that individuals just like the young
couple who previously wanted the smelter down, now want it to
remain in place for similar "health reasons," and the community
of people that never wanted it down and were thankful to have it
still are thankful, whether it stays or goes. I did hear a comment
from a Hurley resident that perhaps the money necessary to
bring the smelter down could be used instead for the community
because he would miss the stacks when they were gone, and
the community could use the improvements. I asked him about
the health concerns if the stacks fell down. He laughed at the
strangeness that he and the environmental group would both be
in agreement to leave the stacks up — in the same way that the
bear and the fish both want the stream to remain free-flowing,
even though the fish would always be the prey and the bear the
predator.)

Turn-in-the-road Dream

In a dream last night i was watching myself in a dream...

the hours passed quickly
as i drove on a lone stretch of road the road
gradually began to curve
my eyes began to tire
then the road narrowed and my vision blurred
i needed to stay alert
a sudden fear came upon me
      — had i dozed off
      — where was i going
this was the moment before the dawn
after driving all night

i saw an object in the road lying still
      — a body
before i could slow or react
i had run over it
for a quick second it seemed not a body at all
but a ghost of a body
a frightening image rose up in my thoughts
as if the body in the road was mine
and i had rolled over myself

as I contemplated this irrational tired thought
formed by weariness from driving too long
there was another surprise
a sharp turn in the road came out of nowhere
      — i was driving too fast to stay on course
      — i swerved in a fishtail and then back again
          onto the pavement
      — then suddenly came upon a steep hill,
          which caused me to accelerate

my engine slowed
helping me to maneuver the curve in the road

i was now pushing down hard on the gas pedal
as the slow ascent began
it was almost dawn and i could see the sun
rising over a distant misty hill
       —fear hit me as i topped the hill
       —the sun blinded my sight
       i pulled off to the shoulder
       i turned off the ignition
a monotonous roar of straight road had turned
into a dangerous unexpected event
and now i was sitting on the shoulder of the road
watching the sunrise over the hill

as i caught my breath i wearily enjoyed the sun's warmth
which brought a secure sensation to my body
i yawned out loud stretched my arms neck shoulders
thighs and feet
at that moment unusual images of people's faces
began to appear before me

was i thinking clearly
       —it felt surreal—irrational
the images of faces moving around me
familiar and not-so-familiar faces of strangers
the sun casting many colors about the trees
the cliffs casting shadows
that turned into more images

some time passed
maybe an hour

—i woke from this dream with tears in
my eyes as if i had been weeping in my
sleep

a memory surfaced
had i been talking to myself
or to some other entity in my sleep
like a vision i began to conceive the meaning
of righteousness
i was tired but there was doubt
as to the words and pictures that were forming
would i later abandon these thoughts
or would they coalesce
and play an important part in my life

and if they did
why now
why like this
and why at all?

Four Poems: Dream/visions from the "Turn in the Road" Dream

1. The Good News

1.

each of us has a privacy
reserved for us
a place inside us
the secret
chamber

i see now that we should be
cautious when we believe
we have a right
to invade another's chamber.

it is good news for i have
my own secrets
my own secret chamber
where i can go and seek
God's guidance

it is between Him and me
what is decided there
what i will do
how i shall live
the good news is
it is not your problem
to solve my problems
or judge me

the secret chamber
of my heart is where

i go to solve what is reserved
for me and God alone
if i intrude on your secret chamber
forgive me
you have burdens
that are not mine to bear
and if i bear them not
i can judge not

forgive me, God, for intruding
where i was never asked
and for bringing sorrow
upon sorrow

i will have reverence for
what God's mercy and
seek not to interfere with
His burden for each man

i have no power to change
only to be a friend
and to know i have burdens
of my own

2.
we all need a friend and
we all need a secret chamber

the good news is i can be a friend
and not be required to take your burden
or to judge you for that which you might bear

to think all the years prior to this i thought
judging your burden was ministry
i did not know my judgment was a

serious violation between me and my God
my actions more than my words
are my belief

if i intrude where i am not welcome
i may be guilty of taking upon my shoulders
what is God's alone.

II. On Abortion (the confession of a male)

what is the meaning of righteousness?

if i trust in God then this is the case i make
that my God can take all the unwanted children
born or unborn and make it right
for the sin lies not upon the bearer of the child
but upon all of us who take it upon ourselves
to judge in God's place

may we learn to give the bearer the right to seek her peace
let her know we care
as we wait for her decision and judge not

III. On Homosexuality (i heard their plea)

i am the persecuted though guilty of no crime
the prejudice against me is my crime
i plead my case—as born this way
i had not the choice you think

i would prefer to be born black in a white world
than to live with what i was born to bear
for black and white and all other colors
do not choose their color and yet
they all believe i chose

and i am forever
blamed for it

> *i would cut off that thing that offends me*
> *if i knew God would be there for me*
> *i have no evidence God would be there for me*
> *and yet still i believe i have been made by God*
> *and i hurt for it*
> *is there room for me in your heart*
> *i want to do you no harm*
> *only to live and enjoy what pleasures i can*
> *within all laws*
> *why not let us marry*
> *and live within the laws of marriage*

IV. The Unwanted

> *in the silence of this hurting woman i swear*
> *i could hear these words*

if you could see inside me for a moment
would you change your accusation against me
for if i am guilty of a crime then you are too

i am as a trapped animal in a cage
you stare at me with a hate i do not understand

this life in me is me and it has not life without me
therefore if i abort this part of me
i will bear much pain
even without your
judgment

can you have compassion on me and back
away and give me room to breathe?

if it be murder and if you judge me guilty
are you willing to stand up for that judgment and
be judged yourself if placing guilt upon me was
not yours to place?

if you show me mercy compassion and respect
knowing my decision is hard
then will you also know that you are in need of
the same mercy compassion and respect for
your own mistakes?

can we each stand before God
each for our own burdens

rather than be quick to make
judgments on another's
burden as if a crime?

— have compassion on me, back away, give me room to breathe

On the Way to Alpine, Texas

1.

where the clouds meet the prairie
the horizon goes on and on
the prairie looking up
the clouds looking down
together a universe

where trains are a common sight
yellow and black locomotives
no cabooses
the familiar hourly horn-blast

where the land is salted with past lives
of abandoned ranch houses
memories with nowhere to go
windmills turning for no reason

highway 90 stretches out straight
a beauty and a mystery
that keeps a stranger like me intrigued
as images of the land pass by
and i drive uninterrupted into the town

the wind landscapes its own design
individual in character — constant and silent
power over all that lives in it
as if to say *i have a voice*

impressions of the horizon as i have never seen before
the hillside almost a mountain
jagged rocks and hills so close
yet seemingly not friends
for they are in it together

mountain ridges outline the sky
their images like that of a lizard's back
many lizards moving and motionless
like petrified giants of some time ago
turned into spiky hills
i am attracted and removed by the picture
do others see it as i do
along this highway to alpine texas

counting fence posts and beyond
the grass bends slightly to the wind
the desert foliage brushes against the pine
cottonwood scatters in clusters
where there must be water
many a settler had dreams
hopes based on a cluster of cottonwoods.

     2.
i slow down to approach the town
laborers, perhaps from across the border,
stand still as statues against an adobe wall
rolled cigarettes burning slowly
the cigarettes the timekeeper
three before noon
three in the afternoon
three before bed
then suddenly the blast of a train's horn
     startles
a blast that will soon be the norm

though i am a stranger to it all
hands wave as i slowly pass down the road.

3.

people rustle about in
alpine texas — slow pace small place
captures me off guard
like an eye without expression
piercing in its depth
i must shake myself loose from this daydream
i am only passing through
nothing more yet
the voice of this town speaks to me

haunted by hollow eyes
i am also at home with this land
as if their eyes are teaching me their language

we are of the land
shaped by the constant wind
we move at its pace and listen to its voice
we become its choir
singing to its tune and lyrics

> *hear the voice inside*
> *we are not empty*
> *we are our own wisdom*
> *you may see hollow eyes in us*
> *we see impatient eyes in you*
> *take time to look further inside*
> *we are content not to change or change you*
> *you are not content not to change us*
>
> *it is your unconscious aim that draws you here*
> *the unconscious want to make us better*
> *we listen you sell*
> *we do not answer*

you strive
time determines fate
if you stay you will join the choir
or you will leave

i must take a breath now and return to normal
what is this haunting daydream that takes me away
takes my imagination on such a ride
i am only passing through a dismal wind-swept town
yet the mirror inside me
says i am the one who is dismal, wind-swept
now alpine texas has become my truth-bearer.

    4.
again the all-familiar horn blast
awakens me from my haunted daze
the sound of the train
coming from somewhere over the horizon
repeating its own rhythm
the sounds of the track faintly then louder

we are the call of the morning and the evening
we are the god of your time
the governor of your day
the sound of my horn is like a friend
you will miss me when i'm gone

    5.
the citizens stare as i pass
silently i hear them whispering as if to my soul
like a song without written word
only breath passing through me in a melody

we are of the same soul as you
living as best as we know how

and sometimes when a stranger is passing through
he or she will have passing thoughts like this:
            — maybe i will stay awhile

if the stranger stays
his first days are like a preacher
imagining that he is interested in us
yet wanting to convert us to his liking
we wait to see if the preacher in him will
if it does then our melody enters his soul
it becomes more clear we are all alike
waiting and wanting for the preacher in us all to die
so that we might live.

            6.
my head is now full
of these unusual solo thoughts
this is only a small town
in some way-out-of-the-way place in texas
yet this dream fills my head
i imagine it is the voice of the town speaking to me

the more truth you see in us
the less dismal we become
            our truth is—
we harm you none
so stay if you will and be stilled
            our question is—
why wait till the grave calls to be stilled
there is peace to be found before it calls
we have a melody and you have none
or if you do, then why are you here

slow the car down man
get out and stand on this soil

can you hear the melody now

again startled out of my dream
the blast of the train's horn
reminds me i am somewhere lost
and the horn keeps me found

when the day comes that i hardly hear
the train's horn at all
that will be the day i hear the melody
of this small town in texas
our god has not been silent

again comes the blast of the horn
i ask myself, what time is it now
i look to the adobe wall
the first cigarette past noon

i stayed
became a part of alpine texas
fell in love with the ways of the town
and the culture
the history
i find the people compassionate quiet
full of laughter
they tell only the gossip that matters

the life and land are intoxicatingly beautiful
i love everything about it
even the emptiness inside me

i reflect back on the day
that i arrived as if out of body
i came looking but didn't know it
when i set my foot on the ground

the experience was a dream
seemingly not true yet real
on the way to alpine texas
highway 90.

The Charismatic

1.

A charismatic man started a mighty church and it
moved the hearts of all who heard this man speak. His
compassion and wisdom kept the crowds spellbound,
and as time passed the church grew larger than any other.
There was only one condition the pastor demanded:
loyalty and obedience to his creeds and doctrines.

As the congregation swelled, those in it agreed to be in
perfect unity, intolerant of disagreements with the pastor's
doctrines and creeds. They knew with strong
conviction that their creeds and doctrines were from God,
and that these doctrines were the complete and best way to
serve God.

Gradually time passed and the church's numbers began
to fall because there were many whose opinions and
suggestions were not honored and who were shunned
and demeaned. But since everyone who remained thought
alike, it was deemed good and right.

Until one day a small problem arose, requiring another
perspective in order to see it clearly. The pastor said God
would give him the answer and that it would come in the
form of the pastor's own opinion, an opinion that could
not be questioned, and upon which the congregation must
agree.

The answer to the problem seemed so easy that no one
questioned it.

The pastor explained that the answers to problems
come from God, through the pastor, and then to the
congregation, and for that reason God would bless his
decisions.

But the problem only grew larger. Although the pastor's sermons grew longer and louder so did the demands on the congregation, and still the problem was not solved – in fact it multiplied. The pastor ranted and raved that the devil must pay for this disunity and more money was requested for the offering plate.

The congregation continued to dwindle, those remaining numb to it all, agreeing with the pastor so as not to anger God.

When the problem overcame the congregation and the pastor, he refused to see the truth for he believed he was God's anointed for this hour.

One night in a dream the pastor saw men debating. The men disagreed yet respected each other in a way he had never seen, for they sought truth as a pearl of great price and believed all opinions were of equal value. The dream remained a puzzle to the pastor, however, and in the retelling it became a visit from Satan.

2. What went wrong?

King Saul could not defeat Goliath till David came and showed Saul another perspective

No one man has all the solutions
No one man deserves absolute authority.

The What-to-do Confession

1.

unfolding . . .
do i give up the farm
because we need the money

on the one hand the farm is a good life
it suits us

on the other hand the money
is needed

what to do

my heart wants the farm
my family needs the money

what does my spirit say
how does it give its answer

as i listen to hear
if and when i do hear
is it God speaking to me
or me speaking to me

and why is the answer so hard to hear
i serve God as best i can
now when i look for God in my need
why the silence

i am paralyzed by my belief in God
despite the failure of the farm
it seems i am encouraged to fail rather
than question my belief

i wonder now if my effort to hear God
is meaningless
i am paralyzed because i am
forbidden
by my christian friends
 to ask the question at all

what to do

if God leaves the decision to me
and if i decide to wait on God
for the answer
then when
do i make
a move

what to do

the crops are poor
we make no money
we are as frugal as can be
up to our breaking point
our children are in need of basic provisions
tensions are high

we love the farm and the land and the life
what would life be without the farm
once the farm is sold

if i sell there is no turning back
though we have always believed God
would provide

why would God tear my heart out
and leave it up to me to decide
and then have to live with it

all the prayers and all the work
have not turned our situation around
we go to the same church and do things the same way
i do not blame God for God is
as God has always been
i blame myself and others for we have penned ourselves in
and not allowed ourselves
to hear God any other way.

    2.
confession
hypnotized and brainwashed
giving praise to God
in all circumstances
walking this pretend love
for God who forgives us of some
huge offense we all committed

we are supposed to know
we committed some crime
feel guilty about it
grateful to Him for forgiving us
then go to church
to be reminded of our crime
as if God would require that of us

we are not to question
we are to be grateful for
the fact that He has forgiven us
and that despite how bad things are here

we will go to the place called heaven
and that should be enough to give us peace

in my most secret thoughts, for the life of me
i do not know what the huge offense was that
would require me to be loyal to a small country pastor
am I supposed to be grateful for all that
and for the pastor who holds me guilty for not conforming
encourages me to seek God for the answer
then accepts no responsibility for a bad outcome
but is quick to accept credit for a victory

when do i speak up that it is wrong
it's not that there is no God but that
we do not know much about God or
what to expect from this God
and what He expects from us

i only see the Golden Rule as my guide
all the rest
        — insisting i am guilty
is a derailment
from the golden rule track.

        3.
decision time . . .
i am in turmoil
over the more pressing issue of the farm
and my family requires a decision
without a reliable view of God
and how to seek His guidance

i must push aside this inner turmoil
make the best decision i can
the best way i can

live with my neighbors the best i can
seek a way to make my own peace with this mysterious God
and not be paralyzed by beliefs
that will not allow me to provide for us.

*(I heard that the farmer took a weekend job for almost two years
and kept the tithe money for his family's own needs. It was enough
to get them through the bad years. The farmer harmed no man and
kept his family and farm; the love of a life that was dear to them
was preserved. So, where is the crime? Where is the wrong; where
is the dishonor to God?)*

Part Seven:
Breaking Through

Paths of Antiquity

1.
footpaths of wisdom
or footpaths of fools

during my walk with life
one day i happened upon a forgotten road
covered with weeds and rock
   who knows why?

is it a footpath of the wise
forgotten
or a fool's path
abandoned

i slowly examined this road
and began an even slower approach
the turns and forks in the road were hardly recognizable
revealing clues of other travelers long past
   why was i drawn to continue?

i saw signs of youths
passing with plenty of time to spare
and the footprints of others in a rush
with no time to spare

   where should i turn
   here or there?

but now i see a turn in the road
well lit and traveled
it must be a good road

yet another fork appears neglected
but draws me to it as if i were made for it.

2.
we travel the footpaths
where others have gone before
we see their prints and study them before we venture on
how shall we choose our destiny
which fork in the road do we take
what shall the testimony of our life be tomorrow
do we dare risk mistakes

footpaths of wisdom or footpaths of fools
only in time can we hope to know which they are
till that time comes the silence of this knowledge roars in
my soul

i am challenged to accept what i cannot know
to walk the footpaths with fear and hope
at the end of my life my eyes will be clear
enough to see the last steps i take

whatever fate my footprints make
whether short-lived or long-
my prayer is that i take
the footpaths that
were right for me

all paths are of antiquity
being that none are new yet all are new
for i am a first-time traveler and all paths are new to me
so it is with all travelers taking the next step
and not knowing what it brings

so i leave my print for another to examine
before he ventures on
with a hope that my prints be of good news and of
some value.

Breaking-through Poem

i am the water from the clouds
i am as i was created
to roll down the high mountains
to join the rivers and venture through rapids
and waterfalls
till i find the wide peaceful river beds
where i become a part of life for all

it was during this mission one day that
i stumbled into a manmade lake
the sense came over me that i had been dammed
for no apparent reason i could no longer move
my hope of reaching the ocean and returning to
the clouds detained

it was not of my nature to be trapped here
crowded in this container with other streams and rivers
i looked up and saw the humans looking upon us
a self-satisfied accomplishment and pride in their eyes

they spent their days as if they were the creators of life
the lake was good
it gave water to the community
and provided wholesome recreation on the weekends
for the entire community to enjoy
so why was i so sad

one night i dreamed of my God
who sits high in the heavens
busy making clouds and forming all kinds of weather
the clouds waited patiently
ready to go on assigned missions to earth

i wondered what my God thought of man
and the manmade lakes below

then loud thunder slapped the sky and a voice said
all that is of Me is My church and all that is of man is his church

i woke suddenly my destiny returned to me
for i am of the streams from the clouds above
though it may seem i am a stranger in a strange land
when the time is right
i will return to the place from which i came
i was made to be a stream
and roam free till at last i reach my destiny

> *is it a mystery then that the lakes of men dry up*
> *and we are sent to flood their streets?*
> *why can they not allow us our freedom*
> *to be as we were made to be and dam us not?*
> *why can they not live in the church God made*
> *and not their own?*

i heard the thunder of God
lightning followed and soon i was surrounded
by a thousand friends singing these words
over and over as they flooded the streets
and the lake overflowed
we are on our way to our destiny
and we come to take you with us
we are going on as we were made
and we are returning to the one who made us

> *i am only passing through*
> *if you dam me and i seek to break through*
> *be not surprised, for i was not made to be in your lake*
> *but to seek my destiny and live as i was created.*

I See You

1.
i see You inside me
as You look down from heaven
You have no written word for me
only the knowing that You are in me
and are there for the seeking

one morning during a breakfast bible study
four of us discussed our views of God
each sure our own view was more right than the other's

and we quoted the same scripture against each other as proof

an anger rose in us all
though we masked it well it was there
why does each of us have to be greater than the other
in our "knowing" of God?
we walk the well-worn path of division
and the justice of making war is in our heart
we seek an enemy against whom to test our view of God
and in this small breakfast group
i was reminded at how willing we are to test our skill
in the ultimate battle to prove superiority
of our view of God against another's

as we leave breakfast each of us feels compelled to pray
for the others' "lack" of understanding
and that kind of prayer is our doom.

2.
why would Jesus not write a word Himself
as though He knew His message
could not be contained in the written word?
the fight within us uses the written word
as a sword to subdue and conquer
and we are fooled into believing
that it is somehow a ministry we offer

my view is that each of us has to work out his
salvation with God
that it is between us and Him
so what makes us rush
to be more than equal to what God has made
and even quicker to be a judge of others?

how much truth needs to be written down
to remind us not to judge each other too harshly
over our differences?
when it comes to God each of us has a right
to believe in God how we will.

If You Are Not as They Say

1. A voice I heard —

if I may speak
the real truth is in you and
I will accept what you find there
if you seek Me there you
will find Me

Why are we beset with such conviction about stories, parables, and teachings in the scriptures? The stories in these books are from many sources throughout time, all altered in search of a "better" truth than the last. Why do we not see it for what it is: a journal by people like ourselves who have sought God and shared their views of their revelations and reflections? May we not have the same freedom to walk the path and see what God has in store for us, or are we bound only to these written views as if no other experience of life could be equal to theirs? Is it possible that scripture is only the testimony of those authors concerning their experiences with God? And, if so, why must our views conform to theirs? Is it not likely that all the writings are flawed much as we are flawed? If so, we have the right to write our own scripture and compare it as we will to others scriptures that come before. The question of errors in all scriptures should alarm us.

> *I am not contained in words but my spirit*
> *alone do I live in you*

I fear a multitude of voices are screaming, "Blasphemy." To believe we have erred in writing scripture is too much for us to bear. We are lost for sure.

2. *My voice* –

If You are not as they say
then we have the right to search for You ourselves.

Can our search for truth be tested
and questioned without condemnation?

Or is anger our response to questions
that point to error in our scripture?

Why do we see this anger as a virtue
and as a righteous response?

Why does scripture have to be without error
for us to see where God dwells?

The Day I Found Out My Grandfather Was a Racist

the rocks were neatly and solidly stacked
in such a way that wind and rain could not move them
the tall figure strong and true
the rocks standing as a memorial

until this day i thought my memory of my grandfather
would remain the same for all time
i believed God approved of what i had made

but as time passed i learned of something dark
— that in my grandfather's beliefs and actions
he harbored a racial bias till his dying day

now the memorial is a shame a sham for me

tearing the rocks down i swear
i will never stack rocks again to any man

the truth is my grandfather
considered himself and all whites above blacks
and any other color of man
it was by skin color alone he believed
God judged a man

my heart sinks as i slowly disassemble this rock memorial
which for years stood as a most excellent memory
but now i lay it down and understand why idols
do not stand the test of time

where the rocks once were is now level ground
and all the rocks are returned to the earth
my grandfather was a man
in need of a God
who could redeem him
i hope he found that God.

(My grandfather showed me the most gentle and wise part of his
life. He was never unjust to anyone that I saw, and he
always appeared to respect others and avoid judgment. That is
what I saw in him and admired. The darker side of his life was
unknown to me for many years. I will always be thankful that I
saw the attributes of his life that served as a role model for me. It
is true that we have more than one nature, although it is chilling
for me to contemplate the darker sides of my own life.
Perhaps the acknowledgment of the darkness within is a case for
defending the need of a merciful God. I believe it would please
my grandfather to know the stone idol of him stands no more.)

Hell on Earth

The only hell I see is the hell we made on earth
and it is ours to unmake

Faith is the walk that seeks to undo it
Faith is not a judge of others

May I have the compassion
to walk in this way

> *to insist on a hell we do not know*
> *to believe it so much that*
> *it causes us to hate those*
> *who do not adhere*
> *to the belief*
> *is the part*
> *of man*
> *that*
> *needs salvation*

Who wrote the words in the Bible on Hell?
I say today that is not the God I know in my mind
heart and soul

The earth is full enough of the burdens we place on her
and ourselves to qualify as a Hell

The good news about Jesus and others like him is that they
show us a way to walk out of it.

This Goes Somewhere

. . . but I forgot where; after you read it, you decide.

1.

how could God trust us with His word
and give it to us in a book written by us
to believe that such a book exists
the root of our problems must be that
the book is our words written to God
what we are really seeking is
God's blessing over the words
and that is the Bible

i believe if and when God
gives us a word or words
it will settle the matter

for now
i do not see that
the matter has been settled.

2.

i sense that we are born
with a connection with God
that the connection is in us
around us always

our sense of God should bring with it a peace with life
an understanding to treat others as we want to be treated
beyond this it seems there are no guarantees

as i see it each of us has the freedom
to seek God our own way

without judgment
and the rest is in God's hand to do with as He pleases

In this sense i can say God is here.

3.
maybe i am over the edge
or could it be that i am moving away from it.

On a High Mountain

i am on a high mountain
not alone

who is this who is like me and
who climbs this mountain with me

the mountain in the deep
reservoir of my soul calls me to climb

to begin the climb is to be willing
to lose all friends for the price of the climb

i must climb away from the altars
we have made and be not a friend to them

not that i desire it to be this way
but it is how the mountain calls me

> *what i leave behind is*
> *an altar not of wrong or of sin*
> *but an altar that lets no one in*
> *unless we are willing to bow to its creeds*
> *creeds that have been made by those who believe*
> *that only they have the right creed and all others are wrong*
> *or not as right*
>
> *all who bow at this altar are the same as*
> *the ones they condemn*
>
> *so i leave these altars and climb*
> *for a better view*

on this mountain i see there are others
like me who condemn not the differences of altars
but only seek a truth where more than one
creed is true and God is larger than any and all creeds

where is the line drawn for sinner and saint
let's sit upon the mountain awhile
and see what there is to see

> *at a distance i see the beautiful things of earth*
> *but also dust from the machines of people*
> *hungry nations fed by missionaries who bring food*
> *in exchange for commitments to their creeds*

> *flashes from rockets where the slogans*
> *of the scriptures of men are written upon metal casings*

> *why do we pat ourselves proudly and see no wrong*
> *in seeking peace with rockets*
> *or feeding the hungry*
> *in exchange for their loyalty*
> *esteeming ourselves as righteous*
> *with monetary prosperity as proof*
> *we are not alone in these pursuits*
> *how is it our self-serving regard for others*
> *has become our crown of righteousness*

i climbed a high mountain
to learn what was in my heart mind and soul
on the high mountain i heard my spirit speak

> *it wrote words upon my heart*
> *where the path up the mountain*
> *where sat the glory of God*

away from the fray and away
from our own written scriptures and creeds and doctrines
where these words were written upon my heart:

"all are equal in My eyes
if we heed not then war and greed is our lot."

Making Peace

1.

I am making my peace with God now
God forgive me

It was not by Your hand I was hurt
but by our own

The peace I am making now is for truth
as I see it

To You my God I hope no offense was done by me

I worship the God that cannot be named or fenced in.

2.

All have a right to You
And I have no right to say otherwise

For me to intervene between another and his right
might be the worst action I could take

And if the harm I do cannot be undone
then I may not be able to make my peace with God

Therefore I will walk with caution so as not to
intrude on the peace all people have a right to.

The God in You

i believe
there is
no race
no gender
no people
that shines above all the rest

i believe
every
man
woman
and child
stands before God
and makes his and her petition known

i believe
God is
not gender
not color
not race
not religion
and has no name other than God

i believe
God is
not in words
not in creeds
not in doctrines
but in us and around us
and God is here

the God in you is the same God in
me and it is the same God in
and around
all the earth

amen.

Waiting to Be Taken

1.

as my spirit waits to be taken
i must live in this body till its time

created as a spirit
and a body
and a heart
and a mind
i am all these things

i the spirit will live on
i the body heart and mind will cease

may the God who made us
aid us in this endeavor for that which we were created.

2.

i am a dreamer of these images and words
i am unsure of their value

we can almost believe anything
concerning a concept of truth
as to why we are and
why the gods are
over us

i can believe the good news
of Jesus but i cannot believe
that it brings with it people
and buildings that
we believe
have a spiritual
authority
over us.

As the Breeze

as the breeze comes naturally
so i believe in You

without borders

You are before the beginning
beyond the end
without definition

You bring me rest

therefore i judge no one for
enjoying the breeze

judge me not for the same

which one of us can control the wind
it moves wherever it wills

we are at its mercy

or is there another way to reach God
at our bidding

why build walls to protect us
from the breeze
then wonder at our disbelief

as if the walls were the proof God is here.

Does God Really Care

if you will

listen to the man at the podium
he tells us that stories in a certain book are true
he tells us that if we doubt the stories
God will bring His wrath upon us
he says that to doubt the stories
is the same as doubting God
but if we do not believe in God
the way he the man at the podium
preaches it to us
then he says God will send us to hell

— the question is: does God really care if we believe that or not?

what about the simpler message
that only asks us to have the faith to trust it

— to treat others in the same way you want to be treated

i take this message over the message
of the man at the podium
who insists i do this or that
and that if i don't i will be sorry for it
there are many like him
they have many different names

choose the message you want
i have chosen mine

i believe God cares how we treat one another
more than He cares if we believe
the man at the podium.

Loving God

1.

i can love God in the way i see to love God
i will go with that and take my chances

i am not cowed by the demanding souls
who insist i can only love God their way
and no other

i have tried many of those ways and
it works not for me so if i am
to love God then i must
venture in without their
blessings.

2.

why are these friendships determined
only by my agreement with their
doctrines?
cannot they make any friends otherwise
or if they do is it only to convert them
into their way of believing
in God?

3.

i will not interfere with another's pursuit of God
how they settle the issue
i would hope that if we are friends
our friendship would not be determined
by whether we believe in God the same way
but i fear that for some it is the only way they can
be friends

— i choose not to go that way.

Me Bowing and My View

1.

i see myself in a field on my knees
bowing to a presence i see in my spirit
the same presence is all around me
all around everything
    or so i imagine

i worship in this way
me seeing myself in a field on my knees bowing
at the feet of this presence i call God.

2.

is this presence real or is it
imagined and if imagined
why does all the world have to come to terms with
whether this imagined idea of God is real
— or not?

whether real or imagined i worship my God
    i make no demands on you
as to how you come to terms with your belief of God.

as i go to my knees i can accept and believe
    as i will
and i give the same to you as i give
    to me.

My Bridge

1.

I am shamed to think the one whom we call Jesus died
for taking a stand for what he believed to be true . . . to
think that he so gifted would give it all away to stand on
a truth . . . that he, having done no evil on the earth, was
yet punished so brutally and followed by those who did
nothing and were unwilling to risk their own lives for the
one who so willingly gave his in order to proclaim that
there are beliefs and truths worth dying for.

I believe if I had been there I would have watched him die,
too, so I am shamed to see me as I am, and yet humbled
and glad to know of the life of Jesus.

2.

I stand on the lesson he taught: that there was a truth
worth dying for. I walk this earth grateful for His stand
and death.

3.

Though I am guilty of the shame I bear, I am free from an
eternal guilt now. The only guilt here is seeing the shame
of our life, unwilling to stand for such a truth as Jesus
proclaimed.

There is no church no doctrine and no creed that owns it.
At best it can only be served.

4.

out on a limb i balance myself with this view
the further out on the limb i walk i find it not a limb at all
but instead a solid trunk with plenty of root
to stand and climb such a tree at first seems foolish

but now it is faith to me
i worship the God of whom this messenger speaks
but i do not worship the messenger
though i show him honor
     — he is a bridge for me to God.

Hello, Fellow Traveler

While on my journey a fellow traveler I did meet
We stopped for a while to share what we had seen
then waved each other on to continue our walk
And as life so happens it happened for us
to meet often on this road
    — *the road of the portals and passages*

I learned one day that my traveler friend
had a worldly wound that would not heal
And though this traveler shared of the pain
she also showed a strength and peace despite it

As time passed we continued to share
what we knew of the road and our journey on it
I ventured one day to ask this fellow traveler a question
for it seemed relevant at the time

She was gifted to help others heal from their hurts,
she said, and to assist spirits to pass on . . .
and yet she was wounded herself

Would this gift within her reach to heal her own hurts?
That was my question and i phrased it like this:

> *— do you sing to the shaman in you
> or does the shaman sing to you?
> — does the God of the shaman in you
> hear your cries as well?*

> *strange as it is
> the relationship that exists between the unseen and the seen
> is the ultimate reality*

She told me that she sings to the shaman, and the shaman
sings to her, that they each sing this song:

when I sing to you
you awaken to my love for you
when you awaken to my love for you
you will never be the same
so sing to me
that I may die into your love
so sing to me
that I may be renewed

the gift is that he loves me
the gift is she receives my love
the gift is that she loves me
the gift is he receives my love

wounded I lie
without recourse for healing
when he does not sing his love for me
my breath and blood stop flowing
their stillness is my song to him
that he may know my love for him
awakening he knows this love and
gently, from the depths of him
His song begins
I hear
His song to fill me

1. *My understanding*
when the shaman needs to arise
she sings to him and when she needs comforting
the shaman sings to her

And though she walks with a gift to help others heal from
their hurts and assists the spirits to pass on, she too has
wounds from this life; she too has need of healing

She says there is a mystery here,
that the shaman in her needs to be aroused
for the strength of the shaman wanes
with each reaching out, and her song
brings renewal to the shaman

> *so the song she sings is for the shaman to arise and go forth*
> *for the shaman's purpose is to perform the mission*
> *for which he was birthed*
> *— and when she is wounded the shaman has a song for her*
> *in some way, she says, it is a dance like none other*
> *when the two parts of the spiritual receive each other*
> *in this motion*
> *— then what other kind of dance could be compared to it*

> *the power that made her also made the shaman's power,*
> *which gives the shaman purpose and brings the healing*

2. So . . .
she lies wounded herself unable
to walk in the virtue
that she is able to pass on to others

> *— why is this?*

> *why is it that the body that hosts the gifts*
> *is unable to receive*

> *the paradox of that truth is*
> *more of a mystery than the gift*

3.

she walks in a place that she sees, unseen by others
— by the edge of her own soul looking out the windows

The sound of the unseen is all around her
The portals of the souls are wide open
As she listens the sounds become voices
voices from the spirits of people seeking healing

— is there anyone among us who has the gift
is it the one who can hear the voices and help heal the hurts

The shaman in her arises to the sound of a distant cry
and she forgets her own wounds for a while

When the souls of the hurting have been tended
she returns to the shadows to tend her own wounds

— shamans must do what shamans do
is she singing to the shaman
or is the shaman singing to her?
that was my question.

4.

the lesson learned is this:
many people have gifts like these
these gifts are not our own nor of our making
they do not need to possess a perfect body
— for that is not their mission

therefore it could be that our own wounds in life
are no indication of the power of these gifts in us
and that the power of these gifts in us is no indication
of a virtue or of a righteousness in our life

is it then that gifts are given and virtues produced by our walk
... that the Maker and Creator of all life places these gifts within us
... that this same Maker is content for us to seek out these gifts to use accordingly?

i believe the gifts are a message from this Creator
... that we are all born with needs and hurts
and that our part in those hurts is to help each other
what better way is there to use a gift
to add meaning to life than to use the gifts
with this purpose in mind?

though how we use these gifts is for us to decide
perhaps knowing we need God to assist
us is where the lesson begins.

Concerning the Poet and Other Gifts

Poets do not necessarily possess the wisdom they write
but may only know of it and be aware of its existence

As is true with many gifts and revelations
the virtue of the gift may not be in us
but only the gift itself

I am not necessarily the words I write
—I am only a messenger among many.

Time to Close

1.

i dreamed a dream where no god had died for our sins
instead we knew in our hearts that we were
responsible for the world we made
all the good and all the evil

every person looked inside himself
and found a storehouse of fruits
that gave meaning and purpose to life

no one judged another for believing this way
or that way concerning God
for the unknowns of God were enough proof
that we were to allow each person
the freedom to worship as he would

there was a saying known by everyone
because it spoke to the heart
— treat others as you want to be treated
— seek to do no harm to any
— this is the way

you decide for yourself to live it or
not but beware, for if you do not
there will be plenty of hardships
waiting to take its place.

2.

as i awoke from this dream i lay in bed
i listened to my wife's steady rhythm of sleep
when i arose from the bed the thought of being part
of a world where we had the privilege
of safety and freedom made me

reason that if any god were to die for us
it would be to bring
this to the world
and that if god had died for us
we would not
still be here
contending
with the
problem.

3.
an elderly woman said to me once
that she could be a friend to almost anyone
regardless.

4.
i suddenly woke from this dream
who would believe i had dreamed such a thing
i thought, i will call my dream *"portals and passages."*

5.
i have been accused many times of
being a dreamer and so it is
— *guilty as charged.*

About the Author

Tony Prewit was born in Stamford, Texas in 1954 and then moved with his family at the age of eight to Silver City, New Mexico. He has earned both bachelor's and master's of arts degrees and has traveled extensively throughout the United States as a musician. Besides his interest in poetry, the author has written, directed, and performed in several plays and as a mime actor. In addition, he is an artist who delves in photography, charcoals, pastels, and watercolors. Art is his private therapy.

For over thirty-five years the author kept a jounal of poetry that chronicled his most secret, inner struggles with his belief in God. During that time he lived what seemed to be a fairly normal life—traveling, going to school, marrying, and owning a retail furniture company. This journal, however, does not chronicle his "normal" life, but his struggles with belief. He believes many people have these same kinds of inner challenges with life, and this journal brings to the forefront the reality of these challenges.

Since 1978 he has lived with his wife Pat, a classical pianist, in Silver City, New Mexico, the place he considers home for its culture, land, seasons, and people.